THE DISOWNED DAUGHTER

A Cypriot girl's plight to marry for love by breaking tradition

DORA DE LAAT

First published by Ultimate World Publishing 2023
Copyright © 2023 Dora De Laat

ISBN

Paperback: 978-1-923123-07-6
Ebook: 978-1-923123-08-3

Dora De Laat has asserted her rights under the Copyright, Designs and Patents Act 1988 to be identified as the author of this work. The information in this book is based on the author's experiences and opinions. The publisher specifically disclaims responsibility for any adverse consequences which may result from use of the information contained herein. Permission to use information has been sought by the author. Any breaches will be rectified in further editions of the book.

All rights reserved. No part of this publication may be reproduced, stored in or introduced into a retrieval system, or transmitted in any form, or by any means (electronic, mechanical, photocopying, recording or otherwise) without the prior written permission of the author. Any person who does any unauthorised act in relation to this publication may be liable to criminal prosecution and civil claims for damages. Enquiries should be made through the publisher.

Cover design: Ultimate World Publishing
Layout and typesetting: Ultimate World Publishing
Editor: Vanessa McKay

Ultimate World Publishing
Diamond Creek,
Victoria Australia 3089
www.writeabook.com.au

TESTIMONIALS

I am lucky to call Dora my mum and to have been one of the first to read her recently published book. What a journey, one that has allowed me to see her and my dad's story in a whole new light. While I've heard their story countless times throughout my life, reading it through Dora's own words, with all the raw emotions and personal connections she brings to the narrative, has added a profound dimension to the experience.

I've always known that my mum had a story worth sharing with the world, and I've been her biggest advocate in encouraging her to write her book. Watching her fulfil this long-time dream has brought me so much joy and I couldn't be prouder of the incredible job she has done.

Dora's storytelling has incredible power. Her words have this amazing ability to transport you back in time, allowing you to truly connect with the emotions and challenges she faced. Reading her story is not merely reading a book; it's embarking on an emotional journey that really pulls at the heartstrings.

I can't help but feel an overwhelming sense of pride knowing that the extraordinary woman portrayed in the pages of this book is my mother. What an incredible woman she is! She had the courage to challenge her parents and her culture, defying tradition and expectations to follow her heart.

Dora's book is a testament to the power of love and courage. It serves as an inspiration to all who read it, reminding us that we have the ability to overcome even the most daunting obstacles life may throw our way. I am grateful to have such an incredible mother, and I can't wait for the world to be touched by her story as deeply as I have been. Thank you Mum, for sharing your journey with us.

Mia Betham

I knew Dora and Tony's story but the scene setting and emotion had me riveted from the first page. I always knew Dora could do anything she wanted, and now she is a storyteller.

Sharon Bellingham

I laughed, I cried. The memories came flooding back of how resilient and brave you were and still are. You have an enormous heart filled with love and forgiveness. I enjoyed the book immensely.

Desma Eleftheriou

Touching, engaging, beautifully written, transporting me to Dora's world and life journey as though I was right there alongside her. I smiled and laughed with the good times, and was brought to tears during the tough times. A true testament to the power of love and family.

Dr Leonie Horrigan

I met Dora whilst we were studying at University and have always admired her dedication and commitment to achieving her goals whilst negotiating multiple hurdles along the way. This book provides a wonderful insight into the formulation of Dora's strength of character and strong family values. I am sure that it will provide inspiration for readers who are wanting to embark on their own individual journey and challenge the "norm" in order to live their whole self.

Heather Mulcahy

Love this book. I couldn't put it down. What a gift to be welcomed into Dora's life, the gift of family stories that shape and mould each generation that comes after. Dora, an unwitting trailblazer.

Jade Toumpas

DEDICATION

I dedicate this book to a few special people. First, to my Mum and Dad, I know you were only doing what you thought was best for my sisters and me, especially because that is all you knew. To my husband of 40 years, Tony, this book would not have been possible without you. To my friend and koumbara Cathy, without you, my life would have turned out very differently. To my sister Angie, for being the constant in my life in the later years when we stood by each other's side through the tough times. The bond we formed when, together, we looked after our parents. To all my family and especially my nieces, Anthea, Marey and Elleni, for your help and support throughout the writing of this book and especially my daughter Mia, who without her constant encouragement I would not have embarked on this amazing journey. Finally, to my three beautiful grandchildren, Tiarnah, Harlan and Nylah, for bringing so much joy to my life.

CONTENTS

Testimonials	iii
Dedication	vii
A Word From The Author	1
Chapter One: And then there were six	3
Chapter Two: Keeping it Greek	15
Chapter Three: Great Expectations	25
Chapter Four: The Not So Good Little Greek Girl	33
Chapter Five: The Forbidden Love	41
Chapter Six: Finally, the Truth	49
Chapter Seven: The Shame	59
Chapter Eight: The Escape	69
Chapter Nine: The Fallout	79
Chapter Ten: The Hope and The Planning	87
Chapter Eleven: Open Arms	97
Chapter Twelve: My Big Fat Happy Ending	109
Glossary	119
About The Author	123
Acknowledgements	125

A WORD FROM THE AUTHOR

In writing this book, I drew on my own memories. I didn't discuss writing a book with my mother and father and had I thought of it, this book could have been richer regarding their life in Cyprus, their decision to come to Australia and their early years as a family living in a foreign country. I can only look to my memories and have them validated by my sister Louisa, who took particular interest in every story Mum and Dad told. Throughout my book, I use Cypriot Greek words that may differ from the Modern Greek Language. It is a different dialect, as it differs from Standard Modern Greek. When I visited Cyprus, the villagers still used a very strong dialect that can be challenging for speakers of Standard Modern Greek to understand.

From a young age, I've always loved reading. Throughout my university years, while juggling a full-time job, maintaining a household, and being a wife and mother to two children, I couldn't wait to finish my part-time studies after six long years. This meant that I could once again pick up a book that wasn't about human resources, accounting, or economics. The anticipation of that book to transport me into another world. I loved reading autobiographies. I have read about the lives of singers, pop stars, movie stars, the President of the United States, his wife, journalists, princesses and even stories shared by survivors of domestic violence and women who have been sold overseas by their fathers. Each story has touched me deeply, evoking a strong sense of empathy and compassion within me. I look at these authors and look at my story and often question whether my story is worthy of being told. Yet, I remind myself that to many, my story is also unbelievable. I lived in Australia, where the norm was to fall in love and marry the person of one's dreams, but my reality was different. I had a duty; a duty expected of a good Greek-Cypriot girl to marry the person chosen for me by my parents. However, I dared to imagine something different. As it turned out, I was a good Greek girl, albeit not the type my parents wanted me to be. This is my story.

Chapter One

And then there were six ....

He who has daughters is always a shepherd
— French proverb

When people ask me, "What's your background?"

I smile and with a sense of pride, I say, "I'm Cypriot."

They ask, "Were you born in Cyprus?"

"No, I'm an Adelaide girl. I was born in the suburb of Goodwood, about ten minutes out of the Adelaide CBD. Actually... I was born in my mother's knickers."

Luckily my *Thea* (aunty) was there to catch me. I can imagine the commotion on that memorable day in 1963. It was the 1st of February, a pleasant day with a temperature of 78.6° F (this was back in the day before they changed to Celsius). An electrician came to fix a fault. Dad had already left for work.

"Do you have the parts I need?" the electrician asked my heavily pregnant mother.

Waddling about looking for the parts, Mum was standing on chairs looking atop the cupboards when suddenly, she felt a gush of water run down her leg. Mum screamed to my sisters,

"Go and get Thea from down the road."

She rushed in and after quickly analysing the situation, started screaming to my sister to go get the doctor whose clinic happened to be next door. There was no time to wait for the doctor. I had made my grand entrance in my mother's knickers. Thea yanked them off my Mum, grabbed me to make sure I was breathing and wrapped me in whatever was close by. Once the doctor arrived, all that was left for him to do was cut the cord and congratulate my mother on the birth of her sixth daughter.

The ambulance arrived after my arrival and I often heard the story that my Thea wrapped the placenta in newspapers and gave it to the ambos saying,

"Here, have some fish and chips."

This lady was not my real aunty, not a blood relative, but as she was a good friend of my parents, we called her Thea, just as we did for all the other friends of my parents. Thea for Aunty and *Theo* for Uncle. It was a mark of respect for those older than us. Thea became like a second mum to me and is still very important in my life today. One of the traditions of Cypriot families is that normally the first person to offer to christen your child becomes their godparents. Unfortunately, I had already been promised to someone else. Thea still tells me to this day,

"I should have been your *Nouna* (godmother) as I brought you into this world."

Little did I know that she would be one of the constants in my life. To this day, I have a lot of love for my Thea Tsappou.

Now let me go back a bit. Mum and Dad married in Cyprus in 1947, where they set up home in Aradippou a little village where my mum was born. Dad often told us the story of him trekking for miles from his home village of Avdellero to visit Mum. It took him hours to get there whilst dragging along a cart filled with goods for Mum and her family. Soon after they married, 4½ months later, to be exact, Mum had her first child (yes, my mum was pregnant at her wedding). From that day forward, she would become a mother, wife and homemaker. Dad often told the story that he had to get his fiancé pregnant because as he was the only brother in his family, and he and his sisters were orphans, he was expected to marry them off before getting married himself. By getting Mum pregnant, he knew that was a sure-fire way to get her down the aisle sooner. They named their first daughter, Eleni, after my maternal grandmother.

In January 1949, Dad decided to come to Australia in search of a better life for himself and his family, initially leaving Mum and Eleni behind. Dad set off by plane bound for Australia. On the same flight were fellow *horiani* (people from the same village), and one woman who was heavily pregnant. Her husband was a good friend of my dad's and he had already made the trip to Australia and she was now joining him. Dad fussed over her, making sure she and her unborn baby travelled well, unknowing that in 25 years, that baby would become his son-in-law. He often told the story of the emergency landing in Bombay where the plane experienced engine troubles. Soon after, their trip continued en route to Australia where they landed in Darwin. The first thing that hit him was the flies.

"What have I done? Where have I come?" he asked himself.

Once in Adelaide, he had the familiar face of his cousin in this unknown country and soon settled into life in Adelaide, South Australia. After a year apart, Dad arranged for Mum and Eleni to join him. Their voyage was by ship on the Toscana which left the port of Limassol, Cyprus on 17 December 1949. They travelled with lots of other villagers, who were also coming to Australia in search of that better life. They were at sea for one month before docking in Fremantle on 20 January 1950 and then travelling to Adelaide by train. When they arrived Eleni barely remembered her father and took a while to warm to him.

Mum and Dad first lived with another Cypriot family in a tin shed until they could buy their own home on Harriet Street in the city of Adelaide. In this street lived other Cypriot families, fostering a close-knit Cypriot community. It was here they raised their daughters. Embracing the Greek tradition, each daughter was named in honour of our paternal and maternal grandparents, each given a strong Greek first name but no middle name. However, as was common amongst many migrants, their Cypriot Greek names were soon changed to more Anglo-sounding names. This was not unusual for most of the migrants who made a life in Australia. Their first daughter Eleni became known as Helen. The second daughter, Evangelia, proved challenging for the nurses to pronounce when she was born, so they soon started calling her Lela, which would stick for the first 19 years of her life. Later on, her name was changed to Angela and then shortened to Angie. The fourth daughter, Loiza was anglicised to Louisa, followed by Maria, which morphed into Mary. Last, the fifth daughter was named Elisavet, adapted to Elizabeth, often abbreviated to Liz.

And then there were six ....

By the time it was my turn to make my entrance into the world, there was great anticipation for a boy, especially for my father. My father, the only boy himself of five children and now with five daughters already, the prospect of carrying on his family name relied solely on this new baby. Alas, I was born, named Theodora in memory of my uncle Theodore who had passed away; another daughter for my parents. Then there were six; six daughters to raise, six marriages to arrange, six weddings to pay for and in those days, like many other families, Dad was the breadwinner and Mum did not go outside of the home to work.

So here I was, the thirty-eighth grandchild for both my maternal and paternal grandparents and the sixth daughter to my parents. Looking back, although the sixth daughter in the family, I felt very loved and spoilt by my parents and my older sisters. And so it was that the Loizou family name would stop at my father. In years to come when his daughters started marrying, there was no option for them to keep their maiden name. The expectation was that they would all take their husbands' names, which is what they all dutifully did, including me.

To provide for his growing family, my father worked many different jobs. When he went out to work, he noticed that those around him struggled to pronounce his name, Andreas. Soon after he became known as Andrew. He worked at Holdens, Chrysler and the Glass Factory. He also ventured into business and owned his own shops, including a fish and chip shop, a fruit shop and a deli. Later on, he took on any jobs, including cleaning roles, to keep the money coming in to be able to cover the expenses of his daughters' weddings, as per the expectations of Greek tradition.

I don't have many memories of the house I was born in and the first four years of my life. The house on King William Road, where I was born featured many times in all my family's stories when recollecting what life was like living in Goodwood. My stories are the stories that were told to me by my parents and my sisters. My father owned a deli at the time and our home was at the back of the shop. My earliest memory was when we moved to Woodville Gardens, where we lived for most of my childhood and right up until the time I was 19.

Our home in Woodville Gardens was a modest three-bedroom brick home that housed the eight of us, my five sisters, my mum and dad and myself. For quite a few years, I slept head-to-toe with my sister in a single bed in my parents' room. The other girls shared the other two rooms. The house had a big kitchen where Mum did all the cooking and where we had family dinners and there was a "good" lounge and a "good" dining room that were saved for when guests came over. The lounge and dining room were divided by frosted sliding doors and the walls were adorned with hand-painted icons of the Virgin Mary, Jesus and St Andrew. We also had many Cypriot artefacts that people had brought us back as gifts when they travelled back to the homeland. A wooden horse and cart, a large *komboloi* (string of worry beads), and even a replica of a sieve the Cypriot women used to use.

Over the years, our house also served as a home for other people to whom my parents extended a warm welcome. The "good" lounge and dining rooms were turned into extra bedrooms whenever Mum and Dad opened their homes to others. Four of my cousins who were orphaned were sponsored by Mum and Dad to come out to Australia for a better life. They lived with us until they settled and found a place of their own. When Cyclone Tracey struck Darwin on that fateful Christmas Eve (1974), my sister Louisa was living there with her then-husband and all his family. Once again, Mum and Dad opened their home and took in not only my sister and her husband but his mum and dad and two sisters with their husbands and families. It warmed my heart to have all these people living in our home.

Whilst living in the Woodville Gardens home, my sister Liz and I went to Ridley Grove primary school, where we would walk to school and home. After school, Mum would always have tasty snacks ready for us. It wasn't just a piece of fruit or a glass of milk. Mum would have much more on offer. In summer, she would make us a fruit salad of bananas, apples and oranges and instead of yoghurt, she served it with cold milk. In winter, we would have bread soaked in hot milk and lots of sugar. One of our all-time favourite treats was *rizogalo* (rice pudding).

Some days, we would walk to the deli my dad owned in Mansfield Park, which was the same distance from our school to the shop as it was to walk home. Although only eight years old I clearly remember working in the shop, serving customers and standing on a milk crate to reach the cash register. There were no health and safety rules back then. I would give the customer their change working it out myself as the registers weren't advanced enough to do so. At such a young age, I could use my maths skills to do this. My sister Liz and I would each have our roster to work alternate weekends with one of our older sisters. I would work with Mary and Liz would work with Louisa. If it was your turn to work, there was no swapping or getting out of it. One particular time our cousins from Sydney were holidaying with us. One Sunday, Dad was taking them cherry-picking. It was my weekend to work so both Mary and I missed out while the rest of the family enjoyed a lovely Sunday out in the countryside, picking cherries and eating them. How I used to hate having a shop on those days, but on other days I loved it because my dad would let us sneak lollies from the sweets cabinet. Lollies like cobbers, fags, musk sticks, love heart lollies, chicos and milk bottles. Some of these names, like "fags" and "chicos" have become socially inappropriate in modern times.

I had a loving childhood, unaware of any other way of life. I grew up in a strict Cypriot household, which meant that everything we did, we did together as a family. Our social circle consisted of other Cypriot families and we went to weddings of Cypriot people and went to church each Sunday where most of the congregation was Cypriot or Greek. My friends were the sons and daughters of my parents' Cypriot friends. Many of these people had migrated with their families and had cousins. I didn't have any cousins my age living in Adelaide as Mum and Dad's siblings either stayed in Cyprus or migrated to England and South Africa. Thus, our only friends were the children of our parents' friends. Life was good, filled with picnics on the River Torrens, Victor Harbour, and swims at Semaphore Beach and drives to visit our friends. Back then, it wasn't unusual to visit friends unannounced and they too would visit us unannounced, as was customary. We would celebrate name days in a big way. My father's Name Day was on 30 November (St Andrew's Day). This was always a big celebration in our household. Mum would cook for days, always wearing her apron, and would serve all the guests who would come to offer their well wishes all day long. One part of the visits was that as each Thea and Theo walked in, they would grab us young ones by the cheek and say in Greek *Xero di mana sou,* translated to I know your mother; it was just a Greek thing. Cheek pinching was done with affection, a way to let someone younger know they are cute or sweet. All I wanted to do was rub my cheek straight away, but I was hesitant so as not to insult them, so I patiently waited until they were out of sight and rubbed my cheek profusely.

When I was eight, I remember my mother crying and when I asked why the tears, I was told my *Pappou* (grandfather) had passed away in Cyprus. I was not fortunate to meet my grandparents. My mother had been living in Australia for 24 years and hadn't returned to her homeland since, so her memories of her father were those from all those years ago when she left as a 26-year-old young bride to join her husband in Australia. This must have been hard for my mum. Although Mum was in a different country, so many miles away from where her father died, she mourned him like the rest of her family back home. She wore black clothing for twelve months, she went to church and lit a candle and on each anniversary of his death, firstly in 40 days, three months, six months, the first anniversary of his death and then annually she would go to church and light a candle. This would become an important part of our family life and would continue with any deaths of family and friends.

And then there were six ....

There were many traditions Mum and Dad upheld and brought to Australia even though some of them had gone by the wayside in their home country but so they could feel like they were still connected they continued on with these traditions. These traditions involved socialising with people and families from the Cypriot community and refraining from socialising with unfamiliar people.

My parents would not allow us to have play dates with friends from school and invite them to our house. Their reasons were that if we had friends over, it would create an expectation that we would need to reciprocate and visit their homes which was strictly forbidden.

Being a parent now, I understand the concern of trusting others outside of our household, but this wasn't the only reason for these rules. This was my parents' way of having us only mix with Cypriots or Greeks so we wouldn't keep company with *xeni* (outsiders). This way, we wouldn't fall in love with men who were not of Greek or Cypriot origin; the only type of marriage they would accept for their daughters.

I remember vividly watching the girls file into the dance hall, across the road from my house to go to dance classes. How I longed to join in? How I yearned to be on stage dancing with all the other girls. I could only look from afar; I wasn't allowed to join in. One time Mum let me go and watch but that's as close as I could get to enjoying this activity. When I'd return home, I would whine and beg and plead,

"Please Mum let me join."

Mum soon put a stop to me going to watch, and that was the end of any dance aspirations I may have had. Other girls would join in on activities like Girl Guides or sports on a Saturday morning, my Saturday mornings were spent at Greek School. How I hated it back then but appreciate it now that I can read, write and speak fluent Greek.

As we got older, Saturday mornings were always reserved for doing chores. My sister and I would drag each other on old blankets down the hallway to polish the floors. The days Mum would declare we had to clean the Venetian blinds were the worst. We used to do our chores whilst listening to Dad's 78 RPM records on his old His Masters Voice Gramophone, which was set in a furniture piece. One particular song Dad loved listening to was by The Andrew Sisters and Carmen Miranda singing Cuanto La Gusta, La Gusta, La Gusta. The memories.

When I was at school, I gravitated towards similar people. My best friends were Greek or Italian. We understood each other. We knew what each other was going through, as they all had the same sort of upbringing as I did. Whilst most of the kids at school brought vegemite sandwiches for lunch, my Italian friends had salami or *cotoletta* (Italian schnitzel) sandwiches and I took *keftethes* (meatball) or metwurst sandwiches. We often were laughed at because of the smells from our lunch box.

In Grade 8, the entire grade was going to camp for four days. My teacher stood up in class and said that everyone was expected to go. He said that all would go or none would go. I remember distinctly the look on my face, exactly the same look of despair as on my friends' faces. We waited until recess (little lunch, as they call it these days). We went to the teacher and said,

"Sir, please don't do this. We can tell you now, that we won't be going to camp; our parents won't allow it."
"Why not?" he demanded. "Did you not hear me, I said all will go or none of the class will go."
We tried to explain why our parents would not allow us to go.
"What do you mean?" he demanded.

We explained we were of Greek and Italian origins. Our parents are very strict when it comes to us being away overnight from the family home. He offered to come and visit our homes and explain to our parents that this was expected of their daughters as part of the school curriculum. We pleaded with him not to come as our parents would think we asked him to and things would not be pleasant for us at home. We also explained that we were sure that this would create a divide in the classroom. If the rest of the class were not allowed to go, there would be ramifications for those of us who were not allowed to go. We finally convinced him we would remain at school in one of the other classrooms whilst the rest of the class went on camp. It was frustrating not being able to do what my friends were allowed to do, but there was no point in getting upset about it as I knew that was the way things were. These are some things we from ethnic backgrounds had to endure. Not even getting into the name-calling of wogs and dagos. That's another story.

Mum and Dad had been busy working hard and raising their six daughters. Over these years there was never any extra money to make a trip to their homeland. In 1973, they had married off three daughters and agreed to the promise of marriage for their fourth daughter. Dad had semi-retired because of a debilitating health condition with a slipped disc in his back. Dad's party trick was always to bring out his X-rays showing the screws the surgeon had put in him. So now, with only two daughters at home, Dad was able to consider a trip back home. There was also a pressing issue that needed his attention to do with land ownership. My sister and I were beyond excited about this trip. We were both given homework to take away with us as we were going to be away for three months. Mum was busy shopping for gifts to take to our relatives. It wasn't like today, where we spend time considering what the person would like. You bought a whole lot of goods in different colours and sizes and hoped for the best. A lot of the relatives didn't have much so they would appreciate anything they were given. Our first stop was Bangkok and then we landed in Cyprus. Relatives met us at the airport and soon enough we were in Mum's birthplace, Aradippou. We went to Dad's sister's house, where she lived with her husband and nine kids. Meeting cousins we never knew was so surreal. We had a wonderful time visiting the sights of Cyprus, the monasteries, and the beaches. Dad was the hero of the village when he installed a tap in the backyard of his sister's house, as the whole house had only one tap in the kitchen. Even doing the laundry and showers were had by bringing buckets of water from the central water hole that serviced the entire village. We made lifelong friends and soon enough, our three-month holiday was over and we headed home. Six months after we arrived back home in Australia, the Turkish invasion of Cyprus occurred. Cyprus is still a divided country to this day.

Chapter Two

Keeping it Greek

Tradition is not the worship of ashes but the preservation of fire – Gustav Mahler

After our trip to Cyprus, it was obvious that a lot of the traditions my parents encouraged were a thing of the past, even in the small villages. My parents were always staunch in upholding the traditions and customs they had brought with them in the late 1940s, early 1950s, hoping to stay connected to their heritage. This was the only life they knew.

One of the Cypriot traditions was that the *koumbaro* (best man from your wedding), christens your first born. In Cyprus, Mum and Dad's koumbaro christened Eleni. This man was actually on the same ship as my mum coming to Australia; he too, looking for a better life. The tradition for any other children the couple were blessed with was that the first person, from Mum and Dad's closest circle of friends to ask to christen their child was that child's godparents. This was normally agreed on before the child was born, and that is how it came about that I was christened by the first person to ask my parents and not Thea Tsappou who helped me enter this world.

Christenings were and still are very important in the Cypriot culture, and each of my five sisters and I were christened in the Greek Orthodox Church. Our godparents played a major role and were responsible for buying the christening gown, a large candle, which was held by a child throughout the ceremony, and a gold cross for us to wear and keep. Small crosses were put on the *bonbonniere* (a keepsake for the guests to take home). The tradition was that the priest smothered the baby with the oil and then dipped them in the baptismal font three times. If you were lucky, the child liked bath time and didn't cry, while others screamed the church down. After the child was dressed in their christening gown, family and friends celebrated at a reception. Sometimes these were as big as a wedding. The final part of the christening celebration took place three days later when the parents hosted a dinner for the godparents called the *mira*. The baby and the clothes they wore in these three days, would not have been washed. The godparent had the honour of bathing the child, washing off the holy oil and then washing the child's clothes, including any soiled terry towelling nappies. Can you imagine the smell? My parents followed these traditions and passed them on to all their daughters, who also had their children christened in the Greek Orthodox Church, me included.

In keeping with tradition, every Sunday we attended church as well as every Christmas and Easter. After church on a Sunday, we would rush home to get lunch out the way so Mum could take pride position on the couch to watch the wrestling. Although a fairly quiet woman, on a Sunday you would often hear my mum screaming at the TV, "Get him Mario!" referring to Mario Milano when he was fighting Killer Kowalski. Her other favourite was the Greek, Spiros Arion and she would yell at the baddies like Skull Murphy or Killer Karl Cox to get off her favourites.

Easter was a major celebration. Easter is a moveable feast and is celebrated on a different date than what we call Aussie Easter. I never quite understood why it fell on a different date, I just knew that if Greek Easter was a week after Australian Easter, you could bet your bottom dollar all the Greeks would be out buying up all the half-price Easter eggs. Now, now, I digress. Growing up, my parents were very strict with Lent; the fasting period prior to Easter Sunday. This meant we couldn't eat meat, fish and dairy. Mum and Dad consumed this diet for 40 days leading up to Easter Sunday while they were a little more lenient with us young ones and only expected us to do this for the week prior to Easter. Sometimes we found this hard, especially for school lunches, but Mum always made sure she had food ready for us so we wouldn't whinge that it was too hard to stick to. We loved Easter Saturday. There was much excitement about going to church at midnight and lighting our candles. As well as the religious aspect, it was the social event of the Greek calendar. All the girls would go out to buy new outfits, or in our case, Mum would make them, and as it was cold in Adelaide, we would be dressed to the nines in our Winter coats.

At midnight, we would all greet each other with *Christos Anesti* (Christ Has Risen). After this we would head home and eat our favourite soup, *Avgolemoni* (Egg & Lemon Soup) and crack our red-dyed eggs which after a week of lent you could only imagine the excitement. The cracking of the eggs was always a big game in our house. You tapped your egg hard against your opponent's egg, and the one with the uncracked egg was the winner. The only rule Mum had was, if you crack your egg, you must eat it. Bad luck if you didn't like boiled eggs. Easter Sunday was always a big day of celebration and rejoicing with lots of food and drink. I always looked forward to Easter with great anticipation. My favourite memories from my childhood are of our family's Easter celebrations.

The other big celebration was Name Days. Sometimes these were bigger than birthdays. The Name Day is the feast day of the saint people share their name with. The tradition is for a party to be thrown with lots of food, drink, singing and dancing. Invites are not given out; friends and family are just expected to visit. Sometimes this party is referred to as a *trapezi* which translates to table. The table was ladened with food that Mum had cooked and it just kept on coming throughout the day as guests arrived from morning to evening. We have many memories of celebrating St Andrew's Day (my father's name). Name Days were mainly for the men.

Men were not expected to lift a finger in the house. In Greek culture, women were expected to obey men and to accept that their social standing was inferior to men. Women were the homemakers and this was extended to the daughters. Lucky for me, we were all girls and there didn't seem to be too many inequalities when it came to the chores around the house. I felt sorry for my friends who had many brothers that weren't expected to do anything and their sisters were at their beck and call. The expectation was that a woman would marry according to her father's wishes and provide her husband with children. It was expected that women would do everything for their husband and be a "good wife". Looking forward, this was one tradition I was determined to change as I started my own life and family.

Christmas was always a major celebration in our house. Even though there were six daughters to buy for we never went without. As my older sisters started working and earning their own money, they too would buy us presents to put under the Christmas tree. I have vivid memories of our silver aluminium Christmas Tree decorated with lots of bright baubles, lots of tinsel and clip-on birds. Whether they were meant to be the partridges in the pear tree, I wasn't sure, but we loved them all the same. I remember one Christmas waking up to find our presents wrapped under the tree and standing beside the tree was a blow-up Bozo the Clown punching bag. I was so excited. We would spend Christmas morning at church and come home to open our presents, followed by a big feast afterwards. In the evening, we would always go to my Theo's place for his Name Day as his name was Christos (so he celebrated on Christ's birthday). This Theo was the husband of my lovely Thea who had brought me into this world. We loved going there as they had eight kids, two younger daughters, Sophie and Desi, who were around the same age as myself and my sister Liz. We always had a great time and to this day we are still very good friends with a lifetime of memories we cherish.

I remember specifically when we used to visit them on a Sunday, it was a constant negotiation with my Dad about what time we would leave to head home. If it was close to 6.00pm when Countdown (a popular 70's music show hosted by Molly Meldrum) would start, we would ask that we either wait until after it finished or we had to leave by at least 5.15pm to make it home for Countdown. We would often win this argument and get to stay and watch it with our friends.

Even though it was 1975 and there were colour televisions, at home we still had our black and white Phillips TV with no remote, so we had to get up and walk to the TV to change channels. We would gather around that old TV and tune in to Countdown each Sunday night. Memories again to cherish. It wasn't until much later that we got our first colour TV, a Rank Arena in a furniture cabinet.

We often visited another family, that of my godbrother Jack. My Dad was Jack's godfather, which made him our godbrother, the closest to a brother we would ever have. Jack had a special place in our family, being the only male allowed to stay overnight at our house. I vividly remember the pillow fights we had. Despite Jack being a couple of years older than me, we shared a deep bond. While my older sisters loved him dearly, it was mainly Liz and I who spent most of our time in his company. As we grew older, Jack played a major role in my life and would end up standing by our side as my future husband's best man.

As my sisters got older, Mum and Dad started thinking it was time to marry them off. Greek tradition dictates, daughters were married off in order of age. Conservative views still operated in the 70s within the Greek and Cypriot community; arranged marriages otherwise known as *proxenio* (matchmaking) were still taking place. There was always a mediator who would take on the role of a proxy for the man and woman. They would be the matchmaker and would normally be known to the family of both the intended bride and groom. This *proxenitis* (matchmaker) would vouch for the family and their honourable moral standing. A man was honourable if he had a good job, had the respect of others amongst his community and came from a good family. Whereas a young woman was honourable if she came from a good family had not had sex with a man and had preserved her virginity for her husband.

One thing my sisters should have been thankful for was that things had changed since the 1950s and 60s, when young girls in Cyprus and Greece found themselves as promised brides and were shipped off to Australia, to a man a lot older than them to marry. Men whom, if they were lucky, they had seen a photo of but most times were complete strangers to them. So, for my sisters, things worked a little differently. A friend of my parents would approach my Dad and ask if he wanted them to organise a proxy for his daughter. The friend would do this knowing that my father was an honourable man himself, who had brought his daughters up to be respectful and lived by the Greek tradition of keeping themselves for their husbands. The family friend would also vouch for the family of the young man for whom he was acting as a proxy.

Dad would often remind us girls to always be on our best behaviour when out in public or when visitors came to the house. The simple task of serving coffee would become criteria assessed by others as a good future *nifi*. This word translates to a bride but also means daughter-in-law or wife. Even as young as I was, eight years old, when the proxies started happening for my sisters, I knew no different and accepted that this would be me, one day.

Once the proxy had been finalised, it was time to organise the wedding. Prior to the wedding, the females would gather for three occasions. One of these events, my family called the *krevati* simply translated as the bed. Other people called it the *paploma* translated as the mattress. Cypriot tradition was that the females would gather around the bed of the couple to prepare the matrimonial bed with a ceremony representing the unity of the couple. The girls in the wedding party, all of whom had to be single, would sew a red ribbon in the form of a cross on each corner of the mattress to symbolise the bride's virginity and fertility. They would then make the bed and roll a baby across the bed to further symbolise fertility and for them to conceive children as a married couple. Money was then thrown on the bed for the couple's future.

The females also gathered, for the *koufeta*, generally at the maid of honour's house, to make the *bonbonniere* (the keepsake made of three or five sugared almonds wrapped in tulle). This was always an odd number, a number that couldn't be divided so the couple would never be divided. The little treat was then normally attached to a gift for the guests to take home as a memento of the couple's wedding. An old wives' tale was that if single women put these sugared almonds under their pillow at night, they would dream of their future husbands. The other celebrations for the females were normally a kitchen tea where guests brought gifts for the woman to use in the kitchen (oh, those old traditions). Although men would normally have a buck's night, it was not usual for women to have a hen's night, well, certainly not for the good Greek girls.

When the wedding day arrived, family and friends gathered at the bride or groom's house, depending on who you were related to. Back in Cyprus, another important tradition was shaving the groom before the wedding ceremony with live music playing and singing of ritual songs. Not everyone in Australia carried on this tradition. One tradition that was carried on was the tying of a *zoni* (red sash) around the bride's waist to protect her from the evil eye and to give her to her husband. The colour red is also a symbol of fertility. Incense and dried olive leaves were then burnt in a silver *kabnistiri* (an item that looks a little like the Genie's lamp from Aladdin). This my father did over six times in his lifetime, as one of my sisters remarried and he also gave away two of his orphaned nieces at their weddings. The incense was a blessing, and symbolic for God to protect them and rid any negative spirits.

The wedding ceremony began with two young children holding a pair of white candles at the altar. The father of the bride walked their daughter down the aisle to her future husband waiting at the altar. After exchanging rings, the couple's heads were donned with *stefana* (crowns) that were connected to each other with a silk ribbon that symbolised unity. The couple then took three sips from a cup of wine and then following this, the priest walked them around the altar three times to signify his guidance into family life. Everything in the Greek Orthodox church is done in threes to symbolise the Father, the Son and the Holy Spirit.

The ceremony was then followed by a huge celebration, with hundreds of guests attending the reception. Music could be heard playing, lots of food and drink. According to Cypriot tradition, when the couple got up for their first dance, as man and wife, family and friends of the couple pinned money on their clothes. The celebrations continued with lots of Greek dancing including the *Zorba, Kalamatianos, Syrtos and the Zembekiko*. There were some particular dances that only men would join in, often with a glass of ouzo on their head or the shot glass sitting on the floor with the man bending down to drink it without using their hands. These were all very entertaining and the crowd would encourage them by making a circle around them, clapping and yelling *Opa*. These days, you often see women joining in on these dances.

All Cypriot households with daughters also adhered to the tradition of providing their daughter with a *baoulo* (glory box). This hope chest is filled with all sorts of items including towels, aprons, linen and sheets for the young woman to take with them when they married and left the family home. As well as sticking to tradition, my mum was also known to live by many Cypriot old wives' tales.

One she would often tell us when we would try to sneak a taste of her cooking straight from the *catsarola* (pot of food), was that by doing so, it would rain on our wedding day. We didn't keep track to see how true this was as I can assure you most of my sisters ate out of the pot on the stove as none of us could resist trying Mum's cooking before it was served. There was always something on the stove cooking, the smells wafting through the house, no matter what time of day it was. I remember vividly, sneaking a mouthful of *kokkinisto,* one of my favourite dishes of lamb, potatoes and cauliflower marinated in port wine and my Mum coming towards me yelling,

"Stop, it will rain on your wedding day."

When visiting, whether it was us visiting friends, or our friends visiting us, we always had to leave from the same door we came in from as it was bad luck if you didn't. Everyone made sure this was adhered to. God, forbid we bring bad luck to the household and something happens like the daughters of the family are left on the shelf and never get married. This didn't happen in our family so one would assume all guests came in and left from the same door.

When visiting someone's home, refusing something to eat that was offered could have been interpreted as an insult. The host may have thought you did not think they could cook properly or that you didn't like their food.

It was very important for grandchildren to be on their best behaviour around elders, especially around their *Yiayia* and *Pappou* (grandparents). This included certain rules such as, in church, you didn't cross your legs or arms, and females didn't wear pants or trousers to church. There were many a time when Dad would give us a light slap across the head if we had our legs crossed while eating our meal.

"Don't be so disrespectful," he would say.

And of course, all good Greek girls helped the host in cleaning up after a meal. The boys were not expected to do so. Some of these traditions my sisters and I carried on while raising our own children, but a lot died when our elderly parents and grandparents died.

Chapter Three

Great Expectations

Culture is the way of coping with the world by defining it in detail - Malcolm Bradbury

In 1971, Mum and Dad agreed to a proxy for my eldest sister, Helen. The proposed groom, George was from Greece and as his parents lived overseas, a good friend of his family vouched for their good name. The *proxeniti* (matchmaker) was known to both my dad and the family friend of George's. My parents hosted an afternoon at our house where the guests sat in the "good lounge" on the bright red lounge suite, which was very popular in the 70s, while the bride-to-be, Helen, helped my Mum serve coffee, *gliko* (a sweet made of fruit cooked in syrup) which you could find in every Cypriot home. This was a very sickly sweet that was made by the woman of the house and always served with a glass of cold water. Mum would also serve nuts, ouzo and whisky for the men.

The proposed bride and groom got to see each other, and smile from afar, but most of the conversation was amongst the older people. Based on this one meeting the couple were to agree or otherwise to proceed with the arrangements. If they agreed, the next event was the *logo* which translates to the word. This too was another huge celebration where the couple gave their word to the marriage. Helen and George agreed to proceed with the arrangements so my parents hosted the celebration of the logo. This pretty much sealed the deal as they were asked at this celebration whether they would take each other as husband and wife. At Greek Orthodox weddings there are actually no vows or saying "I do". During the logo is the time you verbally commit to each other.

Soon after, arrangements started being made including an engagement party which for some was as big as a wedding. The priest came to bless the engagement rings and the food before everyone started celebrating. Helen and George had their engagement party at the hall across the road from our house in Woodville Gardens. There was lots of Greek dancing, food and drink and people came bearing gifts for them. At the engagement, guests queued to congratulate Helen and George and they would make their way down the bridal party line and say to each of my sisters including me *Kai Sta Thika Sou* (and to yours). This would then be said to us also at the wedding, meaning, "and to your wedding" because even at eight years old, I was being raised to be a wife.

After the engagement and before the wedding, the females gathered for Helen's kitchen tea. Helen also had the traditional krevati where we prepared their matrimonial bed and rolled a baby across the bed, being very careful not to roll the baby off the side of the bed. Mum and Dad's expectations continued with Helen having all of us sisters as bridesmaids in her wedding. We had two of our orphaned cousins living with us so they too were included in the wedding party; there were five bridesmaids and two flower girls. How excited we all were to be in the wedding party. It was my first time, the first of many.

Great Expectations

At Helen and George's wedding, there were 600 guests. All guests were invited to both the church service and the reception which was held at the Olympic Hall in the city of Adelaide. As food was very important to Cypriots and Greeks, each celebration had lots of it. These events were not catered for back then. Instead, my mother and aunties cooked for days prior, to serve the food on offer. This often included *mezethes* (snacks on the table) consisting of *keftethes* (meatballs), *calamari* (octopus), *halloumi* (Cypriot cheese), olives and home-made dips of *tzatziki* (yoghurt and cucumber), *skordalia* (garlic dip) and *tarama* (fish cod roe). The main meal would nearly always consist of *dolmathes* (stuffed vine leaves), *pastitio* (Greek lasagna), and *souvlakii* (lamb and chicken skewers). No meal would be complete without Greek desserts so most often you would be served *baklava*, *galaktoboureko* (custard pie in pastry) and of course *loucoumades* (honey puffs). Needless to say, there was plenty of ouzo, Greek wine, beer and whisky flowing all night.

As expectations continued, pretty much nine months after the wedding Helen and George had their first child; a grandson for my parents. He was christened in the Greek Orthodox Church and so the traditions continued.

In 1972, my second sister Angie had a proxy organised for her with a young man, Andy who had come all the way from Brisbane to Adelaide, with his mother to find him a good wife. Apparently, there weren't any suitable brides in Brisbane. Andy's mother was the pregnant woman on the plane that had come out to Australia with Dad and other Cypriot migrants. The one Dad fussed over ensuring she was comfortable. Andy and Angie soon got engaged and Andy lived with us for a while before Angie moved to Brisbane to prepare for her upcoming wedding. All us sisters loved having him live with us and especially us two young ones because it meant yet another person to spoil us. I specifically remember Andy and Angie buying both Liz and me gorgeous ruby-encrusted bracelets engraved with our names on them, corduroy jeans, ponchos and boots. We thought we looked so cool. Andy and Angie's engagement was also held in the hall across the road from where we lived. Guests made the trip from Brisbane to celebrate with them. Flights were so expensive back then that not all of Andy's family could make the trip.

It was a sad time when Angie moved to Brisbane as she was the first sister to move away and venture into a new life. I remember distinctly the routine we established every Saturday night. We would all gather huddled around the kitchen bench where the home phone sat and dial the STD long-distance number to call her. Each of us would get only a minute to exchange greetings and then quickly pass the phone along. Back then, phone calls were billed by the minute and were very expensive which created a sense of urgency in our conversations. The ticking clock meant we had to keep our words brief. We would all spend our minute telling Angie how much we missed her and how different everything was without her. When we each got our minute, we would hang up and all burst into tears. We all tried so hard not to cry on the phone so we wouldn't upset her.

The wedding arrangements started being put in place. My father owned a seven-day-a-week deli in those days and it wasn't easy for him to leave the shop for a long amount of time. He decided he would fly up to Brisbane for the weekend of the wedding and have a family friend run the shop for two days. As flights were very expensive in the 70s Dad organised for my brother-in-law George to drive Dad's bright blue Holden Kingswood to Brisbane with us six girls, my mum and their first grandson all in the car. The car had bench seats and it was different back then, there weren't laws around the wearing of seatbelts. As there weren't enough seats in the actual car, my sister and I sat in what we called the "back back" the back part of the wagon. We had a lot of fun, singing, playing games, drinking and eating, passing the baby from person to person and driving all day long. We weren't planning to stop overnight. My brother-in-law wanted to drive straight through from Adelaide to Brisbane but there was quite a vicious storm one night and our suitcases on the roof racks of the car started sliding off. We pulled into a motel where we booked one motel room only for all of us. When the rain stopped, my brother-in-law moved the suitcases into the "back back" and in the morning when we set off again for the rest of our journey, my sister and I squeezed in with the rest of the family. Back then there were also no laws about smoking, so we would all breathe in the smoke from George's Benson & Hedges cigarettes.

Similarly, to my first sister's wedding, the same traditions were followed for my second sister's wedding except things had changed a little in the years in between and this wedding was catered for.

"Thank God," said my mother.

At least she could enjoy this wedding and not be exhausted from all the cooking and preparations. The four remaining sisters were all in the wedding party as well as some of Andy's relatives. Angie had seven bridesmaids and two flower-girls. We were so excited again to be in the wedding party. A little while after, Andy and Angie had their first child, the first granddaughter for Mum and Dad.

So the tradition continued and my three other sisters also had proxies organised for them. They went on to celebrate their engagements and had huge weddings. When Dad was approached for a proxy for sister number four, the race was on to find a suitor for sister number three, as tradition dictated that she had to be married off first. The mission was accomplished and Dad got to walk her down the aisle before the younger one got married. All the five weddings for my sisters were paid for by my father. He worked very hard to ensure that he could give them the best wedding he could afford.

Watching all of my five sisters growing up, I wanted to be just like them, and I knew nothing else. I lived a very sheltered life naive to everything outside of my own little Greek world. My parents, my sisters, my Greek friends, and their parents all expected that I too would follow in my sisters' footsteps. In my young, uninformed mind, I believed too, I would marry a Greek man. Unlike some of the other Greek girls, I hadn't had a boyfriend through school. I was a bit on the chubby side and seeing all the young girls on the cover of Dolly magazine, the girls on TV and those singing on stage, the thought that I wasn't attractive to men started creeping in. I started thinking that I was better off agreeing to an arranged marriage, so I wouldn't remain on the shelf. I always thought I would marry a Cypriot or Greek man who was known to a friend of our family; a friend who would vouch for me coming from a good Cypriot family and vouch that I was a good little Greek girl, ideal wife material, untouched, with the potential to be a good homemaker and a baby maker. There was no reason for me to think otherwise.

Whenever I was with my friends from school, and then later on at work, we would talk about our futures. I would tell them I was going to marry a Greek or Cypriot man.

"What if you fell in love with someone who wasn't Greek, they would ask?"

"That's not going to happen," I would reply. "My sisters all married Greek men, and I too will. There was no reason for me to expect otherwise. Three of my sisters married Cypriots, who were all from the same village as my parents, horiani, and two of my sisters married Greeks. So, a Greek or Cypriot would be acceptable."

My friends couldn't understand my thinking, we came from different worlds. We saw life through different lenses.

Conforming to the pressures of being a good Greek girl was hard. I used to imagine that my wedding would be similar to my sisters. It was going to be a huge wedding in the Greek church that I was christened in, the same church all my sisters were christened in. The church two of my sisters were married in. The church we went to each Sunday, each Easter and each Christmas. I would wear a big beautiful white dress with lots of bridesmaids and a flower girl and a page boy. My future husband would have his friend by his side as our best man. The ceremony would be followed by a reception probably at the Olympic Hall where my two sisters who married in Adelaide had their receptions. We would dance our first dance while family and friends pinned money on us. There would be plenty of food, drink and dancing including the Zorba.

Once my sister Liz moved to Brisbane at 16 following her engagement to Terry, life at home for me was quite lonely. I was now living with only Mum and Dad. Life was quiet and I used to cry myself to sleep because I missed my sisters so much. In those lonely days, my parents often talked about selling up and moving to Brisbane to live, to be closer to my three sisters who lived there as my oldest sister had moved to Greece and we only had one sister left in Adelaide. Although there was lots of talk about this and I spent a lot of my holidays in Brisbane with my sisters, no real plans were made to move there. The expectation was that if Mum and Dad moved there, I would too and at that time in my life I would have gladly made the move.

Instead, life went on in Adelaide. I started work at 15. My father didn't want me to leave school and go to work as I was the last one at home and he was quite happy for me to go to university and become a teacher (that was his goal for me). I had other ideas and wanted to leave school and go to work to earn my own money. When I went for a job interview that was organised through the school by the Guidance Officer, I found myself being interviewed by a Cypriot man who was the President of the Australian Railways Union. Of course, when I came home and told my father my boss would be a Cypriot man, he thought this was a great idea. My father knew the man, as in those days all Cypriots knew each other. And so it was, that I started working as a secretary at the Australian Railways Union. Little did I know that this was where I would meet my future husband.

Although now a working girl, Dad was still very strict. I still wasn't allowed out without them. There was no curfew to talk about because apart from work, I spent all my time at home with them. The expectation was that I would continue attending church every Sunday with them. Some Sundays, my mum would say that there would be a suitable young man there for me to see. I was expected from this "viewing" to give the nod to an arranged marriage. I would always have some excuse about why I didn't want to go ahead. There was even talk amongst Mum and Dad's friends in Brisbane to think about suitable men in Brisbane for me to marry. More expectations that I started baulking at. Upon reflection, by then all I wanted was for everyone to leave me alone and let me set my own future.

Chapter Four

The Not So Good Little Greek Girl

You'll never know who you are unless you shed who you pretend to be – Veronika Tugaleva

I loved working in the Adelaide Office at the Australian Railways Union. It was just a short walk to the city for those lunch time shopping sprees. If I got caught up and was running late, I would jump on the free Bee Line Bus which took you around the streets of the CBD to make it back on time before my lunch hour was over. With traffic, sometimes it was quicker to walk but, in those days, I only ever wore four-inch stilettos and my feet would be sore after an hour of shopping. I would quickly scoff down my lunch either on the bus or back at my desk.

Shortly after I started working the woman who initially trained me left to have a baby. Taking her place was Cathy, a woman a couple of years older than me. I trained her and we worked side by side for many years. Cathy was Italian, so similar to my Italian friends at school, Cathy "got me". We hit it off from day one. When I look back, I realise that without Cathy's presence, my life might have taken a different path. I owe a great deal of gratitude to her for being an integral part of my journey and am eternally thankful for her presence in my life. We are still good friends all these years later.

I had just turned fifteen when I started working and was very eager to satisfy and impress my boss. I worked hard and during those times this included making coffee for the male staff in the office. Such was the norm. For my Cypriot boss, this meant putting the *briki* (a small pot), on the stove and making Greek Coffee, making sure it had the right amount of *kaimaki* (film that sits on top of the coffee). In that era, ashtrays adorned the desks of the workers and the scent of smoke would waft through the offices. Thinking back now, this was repulsive. My clothes and hair would reek of cigarettes but again that was simply the way things were back then.

Each pay day we would eagerly approach the Pay Clerk and receive our small envelope with our pay in cash. I can't quite remember how much I earned when I first started as a 15-year-old. There was no equal pay back then for females and juniors were paid much less than an adult even if they did the same work. A male back then earned an average of $256 a week so I would imagine that I was earning something around $156 a week. I would take my pay home to Mum who would bank it for me. I was given a portion of the money to pay for my bus fares and lunch whilst the rest was saved for my future. I had no real need for money as I didn't go out to need money to spend. My bank account was certainly growing. Looking forward, this was a good thing as it gave me the means to start my life on my own.

As soon as I turned 16, the legal age in Adelaide, to get a driver's license, I went for my driving test and passed on my first attempt. I figured if I wanted to have the freedom to go out with my friends,

I wanted to have the ability to drive myself. Dad's beloved Holden Kingswood was now over ten years old, so the chances of him letting me drive it were much higher than when he first bought it in the early 70s. Although it wasn't the ideal car to learn to drive in, beggars couldn't be choosers, so it was that, that I learned to drive in. Driving this bright blue beast around the streets of Adelaide, it was a little hard to be inconspicuous and go unnoticed, especially later when I was frequenting places I shouldn't have been going, but it was that or nothing.

In 1981, I had just turned 18 and it was then that I started pushing the boundaries. My sister Liz and her then-husband Terry made the trip to Adelaide for my 18th. We had a party at home with family and friends. My sister Louisa was an avid photographer. She was known for pushing professional photographers out of her way to take that perfect photo of a couple at their wedding. On the night of my birthday, she made sure she took lots of photos of me with my family and friends, including Cathy from work and my godbrother Jack. After the party we headed out to a nightclub. I was so excited as this was a first for me. The only reason I was allowed to go was because I was going with my married sister and my brother-in-law, who would look out for me. We had a wonderful night, dancing and singing to songs like Bette Davis Eyes, Jessie's Girl, 9 to 5, Queen of Hearts and The Tide Is High. I had my first drink, a vodka and orange which became my staple drink whenever I went out, which wasn't very often. Soon enough, Liz and Terry's holiday ended and they went back to Brisbane. Lonely nights started creeping in again.

When I turned 19, I started asking Mum if I could invite Cathy over to our place and if I could start going to her place for visits. Reluctantly, they agreed but always with a curfew. We would spend our days in our bedroom, talking, trying on clothes and doing what teenage girls would take for granted. This was completely new for me. As Cathy lived at West Beach, we would often go for walks along the beach. Slowly, we started venturing out to the movies and other outings throughout the day, as I still wasn't allowed out at night. My social network started expanding and together with Cathy we would go out for dinners with my good friends Sophie and Desi and my godbrother Jack. Dad was happy to hear that Jack was accompanying me to some of these outings, as he felt better knowing that I had someone like a big brother to look out for me. We would often visit restaurants on Hindley Street in the city of Adelaide or go to the movies in the old Regent Theatre on Rundle Street.

At work, Cathy and I joined the social club and before we knew it, we both held positions on the committee, me as secretary and Cathy as treasurer. Meetings were held during the day and soon enough we started planning events like cabarets, social nights and family nights. At first, my parents wouldn't allow me to join in but when I explained it was expected of me to be there since I was one of the organisers, my parents reluctantly agreed that I could go but again with a very strict curfew. Firstly, this was 10.30pm and slowly started stretching out to 11.00pm. One particular night when I tried to sneak in the front door just after 11.00pm, Mum was standing in the hallway, her arms crossed with a stern look on her face,

"Welcome home son," she said.

She said she had raised five daughters and not once did she have to wait up for them anxiously to come home, and now it's like she had a son. This was alluding to the notion that had they had a son, he would have been allowed a lot more freedom than compared to us girls. I remember distinctly being grounded after this. It was so hard because this wasn't like the grounding I had seen in the movies or on TV. There was no set period before being allowed out again. Instead, it was more of a clear message; Don't ask to go out again because the answer will be no. Again, I would cry myself to sleep thinking, why me? I didn't choose to be born in a Cypriot family and looking back, although growing up I resented all the rules I am happy I am Cypriot as I love my culture and I have many fond memories of my childhood and my adolescent years.

So, until the next event of the Social Club, I would go over and over in my head how I would broach the subject and ask again if I could go out. Short of begging and pleading, I would promise to stick to my curfew. Reluctantly, they would agree and I couldn't wait to tell Cathy at work the next day. I really think my parents gave in because they felt sorry for me being the only one at home. They could hear me crying myself to sleep each night. In the beginning, it was because I missed my sisters, but slowly it became more about the fact that I wasn't allowed out and wasn't able to live my life as I wanted.

I remember one particular event was a fancy dress. I went dressed as Carmen Miranda, the Brazilian Bombshell. When Cathy came to pick me up, I had a long-sleeved shirt on which didn't resemble anything like what Carmen would have worn. It wasn't until I was in Cathy's car and around the corner that I took my shirt off to reveal a costume of a more exotic nature, more like what Carmen would wear. Had I worn this when leaving, I wouldn't have been allowed to set foot out of the house. Alas, these were the small white lies that I would start telling. I don't regret one minute of it as we had a wonderful night with lots of laughs seeing our friends dress up as matadors, nuns, and bishops amongst many other characters. I have very fond memories of this time.

My social network was expanding even more. At work, there were lots of people in and out of the office on a daily basis. There were union delegates, union members, and the general public. As this was a union for railway workers, mainly a male-dominated industry, the union delegates were predominantly men. One day, I was introduced to a delegate that came in for a committee meeting; his name was Tony. I thought little of it at the time, apart from that he was someone nice to talk to. Tony, on the other hand said I had caught his eye from day one. Over the next few weeks, Tony would find any excuse to come into the office, a meeting to attend, a question to ask the union staff or union membership monies to bring into the office. His visits to the office started becoming more regular. I noticed he started flirting with me and I guess in a way I was flirting back, not that I knew too much about this. Even after I left school, I had never had a boyfriend. By the time I met Tony, I had kissed a couple of boys but never had a boyfriend. I remember those awkward first kisses. Did I do it right? Did I tilt my head too much? Will he try and kiss me again? These were all feelings girls were having much younger than me. Here I was at 19, only just starting out and exploring what these feelings were all about.

Then one day, Tony plucked up the courage to ask me out to lunch. All I could think of was, oh my God, someone had shown an interest in me. A feeling came over me that I was not used to; a feeling completely new to me. Thinking back, I should have known that with all those butterflies in my stomach this was a little more than just a lunch date. In hindsight, I see this now.

I knew at the time that Tony had recently separated from his wife and he had two young children. I didn't see this as an issue as at the back of my mind it was simply two people going out for lunch. What could it hurt because let's face it, I was going to marry a Greek or Cypriot. So, I agreed and went on a lunch date. We talked and talked for hours and at the end I thanked him for a nice lunch and went to say goodbye. He then asked if I would go out with him again. I tried to explain that nothing would come of it because I was going to marry a Cypriot. He would say,

"What do you mean?"

I'd say "My five sisters all married Greeks or Cypriots and I too have to marry a Cypriot, that's just the way it is."

He tried to understand and at the end of the conversation he said,

"Ok, but would you go out to lunch with me again."

Trying to convince Tony that there was no future for us was useless, as he kept insisting until I finally agreed to one more lunch date.

On our second lunch date, we bought a sandwich from the deli near my work and went and sat by the River Torrens. I remember specifically ordering a double-cut roll, a very popular lunch item in Adelaide. We had a lovely lunch hour, which soon turned into a two-hour lunch break. I found it so easy talking to Tony. Soon enough, Tony leaned in closer to me and before I knew it, he kissed me and I found myself kissing him back. Our first kiss; it was exactly how I had dreamt it would be. The second hour was extending into a third and I said I had to get back to work. As soon as I crept back into the office, I could see from Cathy's expression on her face that she was worried sick. There were no mobile phones back then to call her. She knew where I was, but didn't expect me to take so long. I apologised profusely and told her it wouldn't happen again. However, little did we know this was the beginning of many more long lunch hours. Cathy would cover for me, telling my boss I had been delayed in town.

We kept seeing each other. Again, I didn't think much of it, as I was always going to marry a Cypriot or Greek boy. It's what was drilled into me from a young age. My five sisters all married Cypriot or Greek men, three from my parents' village, two from Greece. The ones from Greece were still acceptable, but my parents would never entertain the thought of me marrying a non-Greek. I never entertained the thought of not marrying a Cypriot or Greek. So, I felt there was no harm in going on a few more lunch dates. I couldn't go out at night because of my strict parents and the rules they had in place, so I didn't think this would lead to anything.

I found it was so easy talking to Tony, whether it was face-to-face or on the phone. I would tell him about my life and what was happening at home and he would confide in me how much he was missing his two children, Michael and Sally.

Chapter Five

The Forbidden Love

*Love that we cannot have is the one that lasts the longest, hurts the deepest, but feels the strongest.
— William Shakespeare*

And so, our lunch dates continued becoming a cherished routine in our forbidden love. We enjoyed lunches by the river and the quietness it offered. On other occasions, we walked through the Botanical Gardens or found some secluded café. When necessary, we resorted to lunch in the car. We both accepted that it didn't matter that we couldn't go out for a nice romantic dinner or leisurely strolls along a sandy beach. We were prepared to do anything to see each other and were willing to make any sacrifice necessary to be together. We knew that as long as we were together, nothing else mattered. Our connection bloomed and outweighed any constraints that existed.

Cathy kept covering for me and if Tony's roster wouldn't allow us to meet at lunchtime, we would spend hours on the phone talking and talking. I remember specifically telling Tony that my parents had organised for me to go to church this particular Sunday where a friend had arranged for a fine young Cypriot man to be in attendance and that I was to see whether he was "husband" material for me. I recall telling Tony that I was so annoyed with my parents that they expected me to do this. He saw the funny side and told me to go and report back to him on Monday. And so, I did. I gave my parents some lame excuse why it wouldn't work. We laughed and laughed at the situation. Many a time my parents would bring up the subject of an arranged marriage and each time I would deflect the conversation. I don't think my parents were pushing me as much as they had pushed all their other daughters because I was the last one living at home. They knew that if I was to get married, I would leave the family home to live with my husband and they would be all alone. I was quite happy to go along with that.

It was getting harder and harder for Tony and I to hide our feelings in front of others. Those sneaking glances at each other in the office. Those sneaky kisses when others weren't watching at the social nights. I started getting bolder and asked my parents if I could go to Cathy's place for a visit, but snuck off to meet Tony. Cathy always had my back.

One particular Sunday I met Tony at Glenelg Beach. We walked along the jetty just like any other couple in love, but we weren't in love, remember I was going to marry a Cypriot. After our walk along the jetty, we were crossing Brighton Road when I saw a Cypriot family on a day out at the beach. The whole family was there, the mum, the dad, the two kids and the grandmother. The grandmother was my parents' *koumbara* (godmother to one of my sisters). I recall dropping Tony's hand as soon as I spotted them. He was amazed at how quickly I had done this. He said,

"What's wrong?"

The Forbidden Love

I said, "I couldn't have these people see me holding hands with you, as I know they will report back to my parents."

He said, "We are both adults. I can't believe you just did that."

I know he said that out of frustration, but I again explained my situation. I had to continually remind him that this wasn't like any other couple in love. He said he understood.

Lunch hour dates and phone calls throughout the day were the most I could manage without being found out. We both agreed that if that's the way it had to be, then so be it. It wasn't long before Tony said he had a rostered day off from his job at the railways coming up and was there anyway we could spend the whole day together. My mind was working overtime to figure out a plan. Taking a significant risk, I called in sick. Cathy, who knew about our secret rendezvous, was supportive and fine with keeping our secret. That morning I dressed for work as usual, took the bus from Hanson Road, Woodville Gardens and got off in the city. Tony was waiting at the bus stop. As soon as I saw him, I sighed with a sense of relief and those butterflies I used to feel at the start of our relationship would find their way back to my stomach. I jumped into his car, gave him a quick kiss, and we drove off. We went for a drive to Brown Hill Creek, approximately 20 minutes out of the city. This was a nice secluded place. Even though it was so close to the city, it felt like we were escaping to the country. There was a gorgeous little creek with walking tracks. We went for walks, talked and of course kissed. It felt so wonderful not to have to keep checking the time as we had the whole day ahead of us. We both said we wished the day didn't have to end, but alas, 4pm came around so quickly and we knew it was time to head back to the real world. I knew what I was doing was forbidden by my parents, but the force we shared was impossible to ignore. There was no way I could do anything to get my parents' acceptance. If I wanted to be with Tony, the lies had to continue.

Tony dropped me off at the same bus stop I had caught the bus at, that morning, close to my house. God forbid, I couldn't have him drop me off outside my place. My parents would have had a million questions, who is this man? Why were you in his car? Why has he brought you home? So, to play it safe and to avoid a confrontation we decided the bus stop it was.

I walked in the door and greeted my parents with a kiss. Mum had dinner ready, as she always did. Since Dad retired, they would eat dinner around 5.30pm. We always sat and ate at the kitchen table. I don't think I ever ate a meal in front of the TV with Mum and Dad. After dinner, I would sit and watch TV with them for a while. Dad liked shows like Bonanza, while Mum liked the game shows like Sale of the Century hosted by Tony Barber. After an hour or so I would say goodnight and retire to my bedroom. Each evening I would listen to my vinyl 45 Rpm records on my record player and sing along to Donna Summer and Lionel Richie singing "Endless Love" and cry myself to sleep. Other nights, I would put my head on my pillow and listen to "our songs" and dream about the life I thought we could never have.

I was feeling guilty whenever I was around my parents knowing I was deceiving them. To avoid being in their presence, I would often offer to work at my sister's delicatessen which was conveniently located around the corner from our house. I would often work there on the weekends and some Friday nights. On Saturday nights, I would offer to babysit my nephew at their house, as their shop had late night hours. I would seize any opportunity to avoid being at home with my parents. Once I had my nephew in bed, I would ring Tony and we would chat for hours. The more time we spent together the more we realized how much we had in common and how much we enjoyed talking to each other.

A few months into our relationship, Tony said the "L" word. I knew he had strong feelings for me, but even with the way I was feeling about him, I couldn't reciprocate his feelings. I wasn't ready to say it back and he was alright with that. I wished I knew how to end this before it got too hard and we got hurt, but then I would remember how I truly felt about him and I would push those thoughts away from my mind. It wasn't until I went to Brisbane, for a holiday I had planned before meeting him, that I realised I missed him.

I was away in Brisbane for three weeks. On my previous holidays to Brisbane, I was always accompanied by my parents. This was my first holiday on my own. The only reason I was allowed to go was because Mum and Dad knew I was going to stay with my sisters. By this stage I had three sisters living in Brisbane, so in order to share the love around I spent one week at each of their houses. I always loved spending time with my family especially my nieces and nephews. I missed them so much when I was away from them. We used to go to picnics to the Cascade Gardens down the Gold Coast, stay at the Peninsula for the weekend and go out to dinner with my sisters and their husbands. One particular place we used to frequent for dinner was a restaurant at Ashmore that served the most amazing steak and seafood. They would give you very generous servings and provide each table with free garlic bread and finish with a complimentary dessert wine. Things like that are unheard of today. We always had a good time when we were all together. We would also spend many nights at each of the sisters' houses having dinner, BBQs and just enjoying each other's company.

Even though I was enjoying my holidays, I was missing Tony. I rang Tony once a week, when I was able to sneak off to a phone box and knew he would be home. How much harder it was back then without mobile phones. He kept telling me he missed me and couldn't wait for me to come back home. Although I was very close to all my sisters, I was particularly close to Liz. Liz and I were the last two at home together after our four older sisters had married and left home. During our younger teenage years, we shared everything together. We used to tell each other about our first crush on a boy, if a boy talked to us or even as much looked our way. We kept each other's secrets. But as Liz had moved away to Brisbane and started her own life, we weren't as close as what we were when we lived together. I still hadn't shared the news with her or any of my sisters that I was seeing someone. How I would have loved to have told Liz all the fun I was having with Tony and all the feelings I was feeling. However, as I still didn't know where this was heading and with all the mixed feelings I was having and the confusion in my head, I kept it to myself. Those three weeks were the longest three weeks of my life.

It wasn't until I returned home that I realized the saying was quite true, "Distance did make the heart grow fonder." When I saw Tony on our next lunch date, it was then that I too said I love you. Tony couldn't believe the words coming out of my mouth but I kept saying,

"It's true, I love you."

"I love you too and one day I'm going to marry you," he said.

"Is that right? I replied. Even then I still said, "You know that can't happen."

"Just watch me," he would joke.

We continued with our secret rendezvous while falling deeper and deeper in love. Even though it had only been a few months that we had been seeing each other, we were both so committed to one another. For my sake, we both agreed to continue keeping our relationship quiet. Only a few close friends knew about us.

Upon my return from my holiday in Brisbane, Tony's flat mate had moved out and Tony was now living on his own. Tony's flat was at Henley Beach, a quick ten-minute drive from my work. Being able to go back to his flat made it a little easier for us to see each other without being found out. We relished this time together, but again mainly saw each other during lunch hours and the occasional hour after work when I had told my parents I had a social club meeting and would be a little late home from work. The number of times I told those little white lies kept increasing.

In the car and at his flat, we used to listen to music together and soon enough songs on the radio became "our songs". Songs like Abracadabra, by the Steve Miller Band and Hard to Say I'm Sorry by Chicago. We loved to dance along to Tainted Love by Soft Cell, and he would often sing Foreigner's Waiting for a Girl Like You, to me. We also loved Bertie Higgins' Key Largo and thought about sailing away together whilst listening to Sail Away by the Oak Ridge Boys. Another favourite of ours was Every time I Think of You by The Babys and Open Arms by Journey.

Before long, we were discussing what it would be like to be together for real. What our future would look like, where we would live and whether we'd have children together. It was then that Tony shared with me some personal information about himself. He told me that after having two children with his ex-wife, he had undergone a vasectomy. This hit me pretty hard, as having children of my own ranked highly on my list of priorities for the future. In response, Tony said he was willing to explore the possibility of having a reversal if it meant that much to me. I thought little of it at the time as we were getting way ahead of ourselves and I kept reminding myself that we were simply having fun, considering my parents would never accept our relationship.

The day after this particular conversation I had a deep and meaningful conversation with Cathy. She could see how the possibility of staying with Tony but not having children with him was impacting me. She knew how much it meant to me, given that we had frequently talked about our aspirations for having children. We both shared a bond over this topic, and Cathy knew just how crucial it was for me to have children. In our conversations, I often mentioned the Cypriot tradition of naming children after their parents. I felt a certain expectation to continue this tradition by naming my children after my parents. Cathy had a different perspective. She firmly believed that she and her future husband should have the liberty of choosing names for their children. We both concluded that it would be best for me to end things with Tony, considering the many obstacles preventing us from being together. However, the very next time I would see Tony, all this went out the door and all those considerations seemed to vanish from my mind.

Chapter Six

Finally, the Truth

The truth hurts like a thorn at first; but in the end it blossoms like a rose - Samuel ibn Naghrillah

Before long, Tony and I were blissfully in love. We constantly sought ways to maximise the time we spent together during each outing, driven by a desire to be in each other's company. We kept thinking of ways we could spend more time together on one single outing. Every time we met, it felt exciting, and we wanted the time we were together to last forever.

The Social Club Committee decided to embark on a Ski Trip Weekend to Falls Creek. I was busy typing the minutes of the meeting, ringing bus tour companies and ski lodges knowing that this was for all the members of the Social Club and knowing full well that I wouldn't be going. Tony kept saying,

"Why don't you just ask your parents if you can go?"

I knew I had to pull out the big guns if I was going to get my parents to agree to let me go. I had never considered something like this before and knew very well that none of my sisters had experienced anything like it. Why I thought my parents would entertain this for me, I don't know, but I was certainly willing to give it a go.

Cathy and I concocted a plan whereby we would ask my godbrother Jack to come to my place for dinner and together the three of us would try to persuade Mum and Dad to allow me to go away on the weekend ski trip. The dangling carrot would be that Jack was going and as he was like a brother to me, they shouldn't have any concerns. Poor Jack and Cathy. How could I put them in such a predicament? However, they were both willing accomplices in my endeavour, and so our plan took shape and I was determined to make it a success.

So, dinner at our place it was. Mum cooked us all a delicious meal and before the night ended, I had success; I could go. My parents granted me permission to embark on the much-anticipated ski trip. To say I was excited was beyond words. I couldn't wait to ring Tony the next day and tell him I was going on the ski trip. I still couldn't believe my luck.

Soon enough a bus load of colleagues and friends were headed for the snow. The bus ride took twelve hours from Adelaide to Falls Creek. We left Adelaide around 6pm on Friday night. We had so much fun with lots of singing, drinking and dancing in the aisles. A lot of the group were drinking all night and were very inebriated when we arrived.

I had never seen snow before. As we drove up the mountain, I noticed a white blanket of snow covering the ground, the trees, the rooftops and our lodge. What a winter wonderland. Everything was white. I was so excited and couldn't get over how magical it looked. I had only ever seen snow in the movies. How I used to dream about having a White Christmas. Here I was about to experience snow for the first time.

When the bus stopped, we all piled out into the cold. One guy was so excited he started running in the snow and before we knew it, he had disappeared, buried in the snow. He actually sprained his ankle and couldn't ski for the whole weekend. I remember it was brisk. My cheeks always went rosy red when I was cold and I could feel the cold air sting my cheeks so I tried to warm up by pulling my scarf up around my face and my beanie down around my ears. Am I really here? There were lots of squeals in the bus as we were also travelling with some families with young children. It was also their first time experiencing snow.

We were allocated our cabins, and were excited to sit in front of the burning fire as each cabin had its own fireplace. We went up to the main lodge for breakfast and were given our itinerary for the day. There were skiing lessons for those of us who had never skied before. I was not a sporty person, so was a little nervous when we went to get our skies. We had all hired ski gear and looked the part, but most of my group had no idea how to ski. We were taught the basics before we were unleashed on that white hill and pushed off. Our ski instructor was a pompous French man who was trying to teach us to keep our bottoms tucked in. He would say,

"If I see any bottoms sticking out, I will bite them off."

The only thing he forgot to tell us and show us was how to stop. Quite a critical point that he overlooked. There were a lot of funny sights and some sore bottoms, not from his bites, but from the sheer thump on them when we fell. Tony and I decided skiing wasn't for us. He tried tobogganing with one of his mates and ended up in the sewerage overflow, and that was the end of that experience for them. We spent the next day building a snowman with the kids who were travelling with us. We had so much fun, our boots kept sinking into the soft ground of snow while we tried to run away from those making snowballs and throwing them at us. Luckily, we all had gloves or else our fingers would have fallen off from frostbite. There were lots of hits and misses and in the end, we had to surrender, as those kids were not giving up. Tony and I then snuggled up and drank for the rest of the afternoon. I was not a big drinker but the more I drank, the merrier I got and the more I didn't care what others thought or saw. Soon enough we couldn't hide our feelings and our public display of affection (PDA) including hugging, kissing and holding hands surprised some of our fellow travellers. It was the most glorious weekend I had ever had.

By the time we returned from the ski trip, the rumours had gone around that we were a couple. I'd heard that someone was threatening to ring my parents and expose our secret. Tony rang me at work that day and he noticed I was upset. He asked me what was going on and I explained I thought somebody had, or was going to, ring my parents. I went home that night scared that they would know my secret, but when I walked in the door after work everything was normal. The next day I went to work as usual. Tony rang to check on me and while we were on the phone Dad rung the office. The news of our secret had reached my parents. Dad said,

"Get home immediately."

I asked, "Why?"

He said, "Don't ask, just get home."

I can't be sure how my dad was feeling, but certainly, on the phone he sounded furious. I knew from his tone of voice; someone had told him about Tony. I hung up from my dad and rang Tony back and told him I had been summonsed home because they knew, and I told him of my decision to deny everything. He tried to calm me down as I was beside myself. I broke down in tears. He said he

Finally, the Truth

would come and get me and we could go together to my house and tell my parents we were in love. I said,

"No, that will antagonise the situation, I am going home and I will deny our relationship."

My immediate reaction was that I would deny ever going out with Tony as it wasn't as if I could marry him anyway, so best to break it off. This whole situation caused an uproar in my family as I hadn't met my parent's expectations; expectations that good Greek girls didn't disobey their parents.

Tony kept saying he loved me and that he would do anything to make things right. I said,

"No, you have to stay away."

He kept saying,

"It's alright, we'll work it out."

And I said, "No, we can't work it out. I told you before, it's not something that we can work out. We don't have a future together. I've told you before, it just won't work. My parents have married five daughters off to Cypriot/Greek men. There's no way they will let me be with you."

He kept saying, "Just tell me what you want me to do. I'll be there for you, whatever you want."

All I could say was, "At the moment you just need to stay away".

He said, "But I feel so useless. Tell me what to do."

When I arrived home, I was terrified. I walked in and my mum was lying on her bed with an empty pill container sitting next to her. She was semi-conscious and Dad was screaming,

"Look what you've done! Look what you've done to your mother! I've had the doctor here; I don't know if she is going to survive."

My Mum was known for her theatrics so to this day, 40 years later, I still have no idea whether Mum took any pills or not. I don't know whether she took an overdose. I don't know whether she tried to end her life. We just never talked about it.

My Dad was saying to me,

"What's this I am hearing, are you seeing someone, are you seeing someone who is not Greek, who has been married, who has children, you know that's not what we want for you. How could you do this to us?" he continued.

In the beginning, I denied it. I kept saying,

"No, no, it's not true. I wouldn't do that to you. It's all a misunderstanding."

I said this from pure fear, fear of what he would do to me and fear of what he would do to Tony. Dad kept going on about the shame that I would bring to the family if this was true; that was his main concern.

So, the next day I went back to work and rang Tony and asked him to come in to the office so we could talk. I told him it was over. He was very upset and kept saying,

"We can work it out."

He finally accepted it was over and left. The next day Tony rang me and over the phone he asked me to marry him; I didn't give him an answer. Tony was eager to see me and see what was going to happen between us. I kept saying I couldn't meet him and he begged me to see him one more time. I thought what could it hurt,

I'd meet him one more time to say goodbye. He came into the office and we found a quiet spot. There was no romantic dinner, no romantic date he simply said,

"You know I love you; I would do anything for you. I have talked to my doctor about having my vasectomy reversed, so please, will you marry me?"

I still could not give him an answer.

When I got home that evening, Dad started questioning me again about my relationship with Tony. He kept pushing me and asked about me going back to Tony's place the day we got back from the ski trip. He again was furious and said we were moving to Brisbane.

"How could we continue living here in Adelaide if everyone found out?"

I was getting annoyed that his main concern was the shame I was bringing to the family. There was no concern for me, how I was feeling, or for my happiness. This conversation went round and round for hours.

After first denying the relationship to my parents, I then told them I had been seeing someone and I had told this someone that it was over, Dad yelled and yelled.

"How could you do this? No-one will want you now. You are damaged goods. Nobody would want a damaged, used bride."

After hearing this, I then said,

"Well his name is Tony and I love him."

Dad then said, "How can you love someone that you've only known for a few months when we've been in your life for 19 years? If you want to be with him, you won't have us in your life. You've known this man for two minutes, you've known us for 19 years, and we've brought you up. How can you make this choice? We will disown you. You will not have the love of a family anymore."

All I could say was, "I'm not making a choice, I'm just telling you that I do love him but that I want you in my life as well."

They said "You can't have both, you just can't. We have loved you for 19 years and you have known him for a couple of months and you think you love him."

He then asked me, "Are you prepared to give your life up with us for him? Are you?" he kept demanding.

"But I love him."

Upon reflection, we'd only been seeing each other for a few months. Perhaps Tony wasn't the one that I would have chosen to be with for the rest of my life, but the more they pushed, the more I was drawn towards him.

I could see how hurt Mum and Dad were, and I got to a point where I thought, I can't do this to them. I can't go off with this man who I have loved for a couple of months, and so I agreed I would break it off. I agreed to do whatever they wanted. Remembering, good Greek girls didn't disobey their parents. My obligations as a good Greek girl took over, and I reluctantly agreed to end the relationship and move to Brisbane. And so, moving to Brisbane was bittersweet. Yes, it was something I always wanted to do, but now things were different.

Back then I was used to doing everything I was told. I wasn't able to make my own decisions so the next thing I knew I was made to resign my job and pack things up and get ready to move to Brisbane. I had been working at my job for over four years, I loved my job,

Finally, the Truth

I loved my life in Adelaide and obviously, I loved Tony and here I was going in to resign, pack up my life and move to Brisbane and that was that. Dad let me go to work by bus to finish up and pack up my office but I knew I was being followed with my every move so there was no chance I could meet up with Tony to explain I couldn't be with him. While I was in the office, I rang Tony and told him that this time it was over for good. Tony said,

"That's not the way it's going to go. I'll do whatever it takes."

I said to him, "There's nothing you can do. At the moment, the best thing for you to do is just leave it and stay away. Dad has a shotgun. He's threatened to kill us both."

Tony said, "I'm not scared of that. I'll just come and get you, or maybe I can just come and talk to them."

I begged him saying "No, no please, I know what I'm doing."

I came home and packed all my belongings for the move to Brisbane. Dad said,

"You always wanted to move to Brisbane."

Three of my sisters had moved to Brisbane when they married their respective husbands and prior to meeting Tony, I had always wanted to move there too.

I got to see Cathy a few more times before we left. Cathy again was our go-between, telling me that Tony was very upset and relayed again that he was prepared to come to the house and tell my parents we loved each other and that we wanted to be together. I told her to reiterate to Tony what I had previously told him and that was for him not to come because Dad had threatened to shoot him and me. I knew Dad had a rifle in the house as he always had one when we had shops to scare away any would-be robbers. It had been years since Dad owned a shop, but he had hung on to his rifle. This threat was a very scary thought, and I could not think of going against Dad's wishes in case he carried out these threats. I could not forgive myself if he did anything to Tony.

I rang Tony one more time before I left. I rang and told him I loved him and asked if I could keep the key to his place that he had given me. Understandably, Tony was very upset, and he got quite angry with me. Dad walked in and I had to quickly end the conversation, and that was the last time I spoke to him before I left for Brisbane.

And so we moved to Brisbane. Mum and I flew to Brisbane first while Dad stayed back to organise a few things. He soon followed by train. He came to Brisbane to make sure we were settled and then he was to come back and sell our family home.

Chapter Seven

The Shame

*My strength did not come from lifting weights.
My strength came from lifting myself up every time
I was knocked down – Bob Moore*

Mum and Dad had always thought they might move up to Brisbane to be closer to their three daughters, and this was certainly a good reason to because they could get away from the shame I had brought to the family and they could get me away from this *xeno*, (outsider) that I had associated myself with. I couldn't understand why they thought the shame wouldn't follow us to Brisbane. It was mainly to get me away from Tony. They thought, if we moved states, they could find a Cypriot man for me and they could marry me off like they did all the other girls.

Perhaps they thought they could save the family name from being any more tainted than it had been. After all, arranged marriages were all they knew. They could not accept anything different.

Dad's grand plan was that we would move up to Brisbane around the time we were planning to go for a wedding that we had been invited to. Horiani, people from the same village as Mum, had invited us to their daughter's wedding. Dad timed it well so that he could say,

"We'll tell people we're going for the wedding and then, while we are there, we will say we decided that we're just going to stay there. We've decided to move up and be closer to our daughters."

Dad made arrangements telling me I was to stay with Mum, settle in to Brisbane and that he would go back to Adelaide and sell the house, and complete our move. We would buy a house in Brisbane and settle here like we always said we would. At the time, I did not argue, I didn't run away, I did nothing. I just went along with everything Dad said and the arrangements he put in place. More than anything I was scared – scared of losing Tony, scared of what my dad would do, just scared.

I wasn't feeling the same shame my parents were feeling. They kept reminding me of the shame I had brought upon them and our whole family. I wasn't happy being in Brisbane and this soon started to show in my demeanour so Dad started questioning me.

"Why aren't you happy? Have you realised now that you might not find a man who would want you?" He kept questioning my virginity. He kept saying "How can we marry you off? Now we need a virginity test!"

I kept saying, "Believe what you want to believe. I know what I've done and what I haven't done."

I wasn't ashamed. I knew it didn't matter what I said, or what I did, I would not get my way. I was 19, I wasn't worldly, I hadn't travelled, except with Mum and Dad when I was young. It was only a couple of weeks, from the time Mum and Dad found out my secret till the time we'd packed up and moved to Brisbane. Those few weeks were the longest weeks of my life.

Among my family, the family in Brisbane didn't know about Tony. The one sister in Adelaide, Louisa was the only one I had confided in. The truth be known she probably thought it wouldn't go anywhere because she too knew how strongly our father was against xeni. Tony had met my sister at the deli she owned and they had engaged in small talk. They connected with their love of music from the 50s and 60s as they were only a couple of years apart. Louisa knew a little about our relationship, and when I moved to Brisbane, my other sisters still knew nothing about my relationship with Tony and what had happened since Mum and Dad found out. They were still in the dark about the whole situation.

They were excited to think we were coming to Brisbane, with the potential to move there. They had been trying for years to convince my parents to move up and here we were finally moving. Once we had settled into our new surroundings, my sisters started asking questions and my father reluctantly told them about the shame I had brought to the family. My parents were so dramatic in their recollection of events. Truth be known, if my parents hadn't been so drastic in their actions, I may not have married Tony and spent the rest of my life with him. After all, I had only been seeing him for a few months, but the more they pushed me away from him, the more I was drawn to him and wanted to be with him. I guess that's how love goes. The more they pushed us apart, the stronger my attraction to him grew. I shared with my sisters the love I had for Tony and they were happy for me. But they were sad because they knew Dad would never allow me to be with him. Not once did they suggest we try to convince Dad otherwise.

Settling into life in Brisbane proved to be difficult. I tried to make a life there, but it was hard as I was missing Tony, my life in Adelaide, my sister Louisa, my job and my best friend, Cathy. Although I was now with my sisters whom I had missed dearly, I still felt a sense of emptiness. I was crying every day. The thought of functioning normally felt so overwhelming. Looking for a job hadn't even entered my mind. The emotional turmoil I was going through kept me from thinking straight. My Dad kept a tight hold on me, ensuring one of my sisters was always with me. I wasn't allowed out of anyone's sight. My parents' thoughts were that if I was always accompanied by one of my older sisters, they could rest assured that I was safe and unlikely to try anything drastic.

Cathy would write to me nearly every day, and we would ring each other when we could bridging the distance that separated us. During our conversations, Cathy would tell me Tony was hurting and that he wanted to know what was happening. She would finish every conversation with,

"He wants to be with you."

I would tell her to tell him that our relationship was over and that this couldn't happen. Cathy then said he wants to write to you but knows that if he writes a letter and puts it in an envelope your parents will probably rip it up before it gets to you. It took a while but I finally agreed for him to put his letters in her letters – I knew they wouldn't open Cathy's letters. We wrote to each other for about a month and a half. Tony then put together a cassette tape of songs to show me how he was feeling. He got Cathy to send it in her name. Some songs were the songs that we would listen to when we were together. He also added songs to show me how he was feeling. Some songs and the lyrics that pulled at my heartstrings were songs from Neil Diamond, "Girl, You'll be a Woman Soon" and "Red, Red Wine". I would lie in bed at night crying listening to the songs he had compiled for me. Resonating with the lyrics of songs like "Only the Lonely" and "You'll Never Find Another Love Like Mine" I wondered if Tony and I would ever be reunited.

In the meantime, I accompanied my parents and sisters to the wedding of this friend of ours. I was watching the newly married couple, on the dance floor, who had earlier declared their love for each other, and that's what got me thinking, hang on a minute, that could be Tony and I. This Cypriot girl married an older guy who was half- Greek, a divorcee and had a child. So, this got me thinking that perhaps this could be the potential destiny for Tony and me as well. If this Cypriot bride could get her parents to accept this union then why couldn't I? At this moment, at the wedding, a sense of empowerment came over me, and it was then that I thought I could accomplish the same for us.

Contemplating a decision to return home and reunite with Tony, I recognised Dad would undoubtedly perceive it as another instance of me bringing more shame to the family. My biggest challenge was Dad's looming trip back to Adelaide by train to sell our house and relocate our belongings up to Brisbane. If I was making the decision to go back, I didn't want to be the cause or the catalyst for them selling our family home. I didn't want them to blame me for selling their home when I had been thinking of moving back to Adelaide. This was playing heavily on my mind. I resolved that if I were to return, I had to do so before my father left. I wanted him to see that I was serious about moving back and then it was his choice whether they lived in Brisbane or Adelaide. My aim was to ensure that their house sale wasn't attributed to my actions. Throughout this process, the idea of disclosing my intentions to them never crossed my mind. I knew fully that discussing my plans would only lead to resistance. I was scared that my father's threats would become a reality and that someone would get hurt.

Lurking in the back of my mind was the thought that good Greek girls don't leave home before they are married. If I went back to Adelaide, I didn't want to move in with Tony. I was determined not to provide my parents with the satisfaction of saying that I was living in sin, and that I was bringing shame to the family yet again. This was weighing heavily on my mind and kept clouding my judgement when considering my options. My determination to go against expectations while trying to balance with tradition was an ongoing struggle.

I finally decided to go back home; however, the specifics of when and how to carry out my plan remained uncertain. I confided in my sister Louisa that I was planning on coming back home. She was prepared to help me by giving me a roof over my head. Mick, her husband at the time, agreed to allow me to stay at their house, but there was one obstacle in the way. Mick was willing to assist and support me, but out of respect for my mum and dad, he was reluctant to have Tony at their home. He was supportive of my decision, but set the condition that Tony wouldn't be allowed to visit me. Nevertheless, he wouldn't stop me from seeing Tony.

I was always a very well-organised person. In everything I did, I made lists. The first thing on my list, a place to live, tick. With that sorted, I moved on to the next task. My immediate priority was to let Tony know I had made my decision to come back. I told one of my sisters I was going for a walk. I walked as fast as I could to a phone box and rang Tony to tell him I was coming home. There were no mobile phones back then and I couldn't ring him from my sister's place, risking someone overhearing our conversation. I rang and said that I had made up my mind, I would come back, but I needed time to do a few things and sort some things out. This call marked the turning point, setting in motion the next chapter of my journey.

Louisa, Mick, Tony and Cathy were the only ones who knew that I was putting something in place. I didn't have access to a lot of money, but I had some in my account. I had considered turning up at the airport on the day and securing a last-minute flight, but being as organised as I liked to be I actually booked an early morning flight with TAA (a now-defunct airline). Mum and Dad were staying at one of my sister's houses and I was staying at one of the others. This one particular morning, I had a small bag packed with a few of my things and was ready to walk out the door and make my way to a taxi rank that I had cased out a few days before. I was heading for the airport to get on my booked flight. What I didn't count on was my sister waking up. No matter how quietly I tried heading down the stairs, I woke my sister. This sister would never go against my parents' wishes and although she wanted me to be happy, in her eyes there was no excuse for disobeying our parents.

"Where do you think you're going?" she asked obviously very annoyed. "What are you doing?"

"I'm going to the airport, I've got to go back, I can't do this, I can't live here, I'm going back to Adelaide."

She was not impressed. Although it was 6.00am, she made me get straight in her car and drove me to Liz's where Mum and Dad were staying. When we got there, she said,

"Here's your daughter. I don't want her staying with me. Do you know what I found her doing? She was creeping out to go to the airport to go back to Adelaide. So here, have her!" She looked at me and said, "You can stay here. I don't want you back at my place."

This enraged my father to no end. He grabbed a kitchen chair and threatened to smash it over my head. Screaming at me, he said,

"I told you I'm going to Adelaide to sell the house. What are you doing? Are you going to stay here or are you going to go back to Adelaide?"

I kept saying, "I'm going back to Adelaide."

Somehow, in that short time since moving to Brisbane, I found the strength to fight back. But he still wouldn't listen. Whilst holding the chair over my head, he kept saying,

"I want you to tell me that you're staying here with your mother! You tell me that or I'll break this over your head!"

That's when Liz was screaming,

"Dad! Dad, what are you doing? Stop doing this! You will wake my baby."

Dad continued with his yelling and then Liz screamed back,

"My baby, my baby's crying."

Liz's two-year-old daughter started crying and she couldn't settle her and then Liz was crying uncontrollably and it's only that they were crying that Dad stopped. Things settled down a bit and Dad thought that he had scared me enough to change my mind and stay. Dad was booked on a train leaving that day. He cancelled his booking so he could stay and ensure I wasn't going anywhere.

It was after that event that I spoke more about my feelings to my sisters. Two of them were happy for me that I had fallen in love and that I didn't want to be in an arranged marriage. They both said if you choose to leave and be with him, we will support you, but this was only to a certain extent. They weren't prepared to go into a fight against my parents, even though they were married women, set up in their own houses. They weren't prepared to openly help me achieve my goal. Understandably, they wanted to remain in the good books with Mum and Dad. So when I eventually made up my mind that I was going to go back to Adelaide to be with Tony, I didn't tell them.

Soon after the event with the chair, Dad left by train to go to Adelaide. I can't recall whether I finally gave in and said I would stay, but in my mind, I was planning my escape. I knew the train from Brisbane to Adelaide would take around three days so I knew I had three days to get back to Adelaide to show him I was serious and for him to understand that I didn't want him to sell our family home and blame me. I didn't want Dad to say,

"You made us sell our house and now you are moving back to Adelaide. We could have stayed in Adelaide." That's all that was going through my head.

Chapter Eight

The Escape

When the world says "Give up", hope whispers "Try it One More Time" - Author unknown

I faced the task of figuring out my next steps. I needed to put a plan in place. Contacting Tony directly was out of the question, given that I was being watched like a hawk. So, I reached out to Cathy. I told her,

"Cathy, you need to let Tony know I didn't catch my flight, but tell him that missing it has only strengthened my determination to come back. I can't predict when or how, but I'm committed to making it happen."

I was at my sister Liz's house, and my mum was there. I don't know why, but on this day guests were visiting all day. Mum was entertaining guests downstairs and I recall being upstairs in my room. Liz's house was a double-story home that had external stairs from the second floor that could get you down into the backyard where there was a side gate. While my mum was distracted by the guests, I thought I would attempt my escape. I would go down the back stairs, out the side gate, cross the road to the Carindale Shopping Centre, where I knew there was a taxi rank and get myself to the airport. This time, I decided I wouldn't even attempt to pack a bag and take any of my belongings. As long as I had my handbag, which had some money for a taxi fare and a flight, that's all I needed. There was just one glitch in my elaborate plan. Every time my mum was downstairs, and I was upstairs ready to make my escape, my handbag was downstairs. I recall thinking, ok I'll go downstairs and wait for Mum to go upstairs to make coffee as Liz's kitchen was upstairs.

I had said to my sister Liz earlier,

"You know I'm going to do this; I'm going to go. I can't stay."

Liz was supportive and happy for me and what I was going to do with my life, but again she said,

"I don't want to hear it, you just do it. We'll deal with it after. I don't want to know. I can't help you and the less I know, the better. I don't want to lie to Mum and Dad."

This meant I was on my own. My sisters in Brisbane weren't willing to help me get back to Adelaide. I was so grateful that Louisa was willing to help me.

So, this day, every time I was upstairs and Mum was downstairs or vice versa, I would think I could do this. It seemed like it took the whole day to get to where I was upstairs with my handbag in tow and Mum was downstairs. It finally worked out. My heart was beating so fast. I crept down those external stairs and opened the wooden gate, hoping to God it wouldn't creak and I'd be found out. I ran as fast as I could, adrenaline pumping, and jumped in the first taxi at the head of the taxi rank. I said,

"To the airport please." The taxi driver looked at me and said,

"Where's your luggage?"

"I don't have any," I said.

"Gee, you're the first woman I know that travels that lightly," he said.

I was in no mood for jokes, but he didn't know that, so I just smiled. The entire trip to the airport I kept looking over my shoulder, wondering whether Mum had realised I was gone and checking to see if anybody was following me. Once at the airport, I paid the taxi driver and went into the terminal. I didn't know what to do. I went to the ticket counter and purchased a one-way ticket to Adelaide. I then found a public phone and rang Louisa and told her I was at the airport. I asked her to tell her husband Mick to go to our house and take Dad's rifle and hide it, which he did.

I then rang Tony and said,

"I'm at the airport. I'm scared. I'm not sure what to do?"

He told me that Louisa had rung him and said that Mum was on her way to the airport. My sister had rung Louisa and said,

"Dora's missing. We think she's gone to the airport. Mum is getting on a plane; can you pick her up?"

By this stage, I was feeling pretty stressed and started crying saying to Tony,

"What should I do, I'm scared?"

"Go and find the Federal Police and tell them what's happening and they'll look out for you," he said.

And so that is what I did. The Federal Police took me into a private room. They were very helpful but asked lots and lots of questions. I tried to answer in between my tears.

"What's happening?" they asked.

"I'm 19, I'm going home to Adelaide to my boyfriend. Pretty sure he will be at the airport waiting for me. My father is on a train going to Adelaide, if he hears that I'm going back to Adelaide there's every chance that he'll have someone there at the airport waiting to pick me up and take me to their place to keep me away from my boyfriend. He has threatened to kill me and my boyfriend."

The Federal Police stayed with me until it was time for me to board my plane. They escorted me onto the tarmac.

At this stage, I was very upset, overwhelmed, and distressed. As I stepped onto the tarmac with a police escort, my sister broke through security and rushed towards me, pleading with me to reconsider what I was doing. She ran out and grabbed me and pulled me down to the ground. She started screaming,

"Don't do this! You know what's going to happen, Dad's going to kill you, don't do this, don't go please Dora don't go!"

As she was grabbing me, I stumbled and fell to the ground, scraping my knees; I started bleeding. The police intervened and took her away. By this stage, I was distraught. I boarded the plane. I remember sitting near the front. Tears streaming down my face. No matter how hard I tried to compose myself and stop crying, I couldn't. A compassionate lady sitting next to me asked,

The Escape

"Are you alright love? Oh, you're bleeding. Do you need something? Don't you like flying? Are you ok? Can I get you something?"

Through my tears, I said I was fine and continued to cry all the way to Adelaide.

Even now, forty years later, I still can't say with absolute certainty, but I believe strongly that my mum and I were on the same plane that day. The circumstances suggest it, although I can't confirm it definitively. As we landed, I became anxious, although I didn't know Mum was on the same plane. I was nervous about what or who would be awaiting me. Mick and Louisa, my brother-in-law and sister, arrived at the airport in separate cars. One of them was taking me to their home, while the other was waiting to take Mum to her place.

Once I got to Adelaide, I didn't know what to expect. The Federal Police were waiting at the airport to escort me to safety. Their presence added another layer of anxiousness. In those critical moments, their watchful eyes and vigilant presence offered both reassurance and a chilling reminder of the danger that had prompted my escape.

I noticed Tony and Cathy standing at a distance within the airport premises. Their unwavering support was evident, though they maintained a discreet distance, fully aware of the gravity of the situation. Their watchful yet unobtrusive presence mirrored the conflicting emotions I was feeling - the worry of my unknown future combined with the support of loved ones who stood by, ready to lend a hand in whatever way they could. They were watching from afar but didn't interfere with what was happening.

Once again, the adrenalin was pumping. I was nervous through the whole thing. Even when the police were with me, and I was waiting for Louisa, they were saying to me,

"Are you going to be alright?"

"I don't know. I don't know if my dad has sent anyone to grab me and take me away, I don't know. I'm just waiting for my sister."

I'm not sure how Louisa found me, but I had told her I was going to go seek the assistance of the Federal Police. She must have looked for them at the airport. We weren't sure what to expect at the airport. I was so relieved when I saw my sister. We quickly hugged, and she whisked me away to her car while Mick waited for Mum to get off the plane. Mick took Mum home to her house. It was in the car park I saw Tony and Cathy. I ran to Tony, and we hugged for a few minutes, and then I quickly hugged Cathy and told them I would speak to them both tomorrow. Louisa then took me to her house. The next day, Dad arrived home by train. The train took three days from Brisbane to Adelaide and my goal was to get to Adelaide before him. My mission was complete.

Louisa's house was always like Fort Knox. They had a front door with a deadlock and they had a window next to it with another deadlock and you could open it to see who was at the door. We arranged for anyone like Tony or Cathy who wanted to ring me to ring twice and hang up before they rang the third time. I would then pick up and talk to them. I wasn't ready to have a conversation with my mum or dad at this stage. The day my dad arrived back home, I remember him coming to Louisa's house. I was on my own as Louisa was at work at the deli so I opened the window and Dad kept saying,

"What, are you scared of your father? Aren't you going to let me in?"

I was scared, and I wasn't going to let him in. By this stage, he was screaming at me. I can't remember exactly what he was saying, but the same sorts of comments as I had heard before.

"You are bringing more shame to our family. Stop this nonsense. Come home and let's go back to Brisbane."

The Escape

Having made my escape and now back on home soil, there was no way I was going to do as he asked. Not sure where I found the strength, but I said no and closed the door to the window.

Dad eventually left, and I rang Louisa straight away. She went to my parents' home and asked what Dad wanted. Thinking back, Louisa was very brave to face up to my dad and tell him Dora wasn't coming home. Dad told Louisa that he was organising a mediation of sorts. He said that he wanted to bring the priest and a support person, his koumbaro, to a meeting to discuss the situation. He asked Louisa to tell Tony to come as well and to bring his father. Tony was 32, had been married, divorced and living out of home for over ten years and he was asked to bring his father. In order to appease Dad, Louisa said she would see what she could organise. Louisa came home and told me what Dad wanted. I rang Tony and he couldn't believe that he had to bring his dad to this meeting, but he was prepared to do anything to make this right.

This was the second day after I had arrived back and the first day after Dad had arrived, so he was not wasting any time to get this sorted. So, this meeting was to be held between the men and me. Louisa and Mum weren't to be involved, but they were in the kitchen, making coffee, as good Greek women do.

From what I recall, the priest started the conversation telling us that Dad was upset as he expected me to marry a Cypriot or Greek man. In the beginning, the conversation was civil. My Dad asked Tony's dad what he thought of the situation and he said,

"As long as they are happy, then I am happy."

Dad's koumbaro asserted,

"We're Cypriots, we do things different to you Australians"

Disregarding the fact Tony and his father were also immigrants originally from the Netherlands. He emphasised Greek customs of sitting down for dinner as a close-knit family, listening to Greek music, and preserving our Greek traditions. His claim to our Greek identity became strong because there was a threat to bringing in an outsider. This man then directed a personal question towards me. He had obviously done his own digging and found out some information about Tony. He directed his question at me saying,

"Why would you want to marry a man that can't give you babies?"

He then said something ludicrous insinuating that Tony's lack of chest hair made him less of a man. He said,

"Why would you want to marry a man that has no hair on his chest? He's not a man, he's never going to be a man. He won't be able to father any children."

This man seemed unaware that Tony had already fathered two children. I just couldn't believe he would stoop this low to get his point across. Thankfully, the priest was very calm and quickly put a stop to this nonsense.

Tony and his father sat in silence, listening and allowing the others to share their thoughts. Eventually, Tony said,

"None of that truly matters. What does matter is that I deeply care for Dora, and I believe we have a future together. That's what counts."

Mum was not meant to be a part of the meeting. She was in the kitchen with Louisa but she turned up with a walking stick which she had never needed before now. I was sure this was for effect. She started waving the walking stick around screaming at me,

"You're killing me. Look what you are doing to me." She then put a curse on Tony. I don't recall the exact words she used.

The Escape

There was no resolution to the meeting. In the end, Tony and I said that we would see where our relationship took us. We weren't prepared to say it was going to end, and that's where we left the meeting. The very next day Dad put the house on the market and soon after moved to Queensland again to get away from the embarrassment of his daughter and the shame I had brought to the family.

The next day I ticked off another thing off my list and I organised to get my job back. My boss was happy to have me. In the meantime, I was still helping Mick and Louisa at their deli on weekends. This one particular day, this same man that was at the meeting came into the shop and said to me,

"Why are you doing this to your parents? Why are you going to make a life with a man who is not going to be able to give you children?"

He had this fascination with Tony's chest hair. I'm not sure whether it's a proven fact that men with no chest hair are not manly and can't father children. Tony already had two children and I am sure he had little chest hair when he fathered them, so I couldn't see the connection. Alas, everyone is entitled to their own opinion.

Whilst I was in Brisbane, Tony kept a diary which he shared with me upon my return. Tony started writing in his diary on 4 September 1982 but he states in there that he needed to recount the days up till then to satisfy his own mind and to clarify the situation of his life to anyone who might read this any time in the future. He started the diary on 23 August; the day we returned from the ski trip. After spending some time together at Tony's place that morning he took me home. He recounted what a wonderful time we had on the ski trip and the last morning we had together. Tony wrote in his diary for 54 days; a period he says was the hardest time he ever had to live through. His last entry was on 17 October 1982, where he states, "Dora has agreed to marry me."

This Disowned Daughter

Quoting from Tony's diary, the first entry is his daily prayer, which he took from his favourite author Stephen King. The prayer reads:

> *God grant me the SERENITY to accept what I cannot change the TENACITY to change what I may and the GOOD LUCK not to f*** up too often.*
>
> Stephen King, book Salem's Lot

He follows this with:

> *I write this diary in the interest of self-preservation to stop myself going out of my mind. Never before in my life have I felt the way I do now. Never before have I felt so useless, never before have I missed someone as much as I miss Dora and never before has my life been so empty.*
>
> *May God grant me absolution for my sins and answer my prayer return Dora to me Lord for we are both your children. Let us be happy in each other and in your kingdom, God please answer my prayer.*

I was saddened to read in Tony's diary that during my absence, he experienced bouts of depression. He contemplated ending his own life. He took some pills and laid on his bed and waited patiently. Fortunately, God had other plans for him.

Chapter Nine

The Fallout

Strong women aren't simply born. They are made by the storms they walk through – Author unknown

Mum and Dad moved to Brisbane in the October 1982 and moved in with one of my sisters. They settled into life in Brisbane without me. They embarked on a new chapter of their life, adjusting to a new city, a new state, and a life without me. From what I have been told, their demeanour had shifted to one of sorrow and sadness. They could not find a way out of this dark space they now found themselves in. They didn't socialise and acted as if they were in mourning. Perhaps, in their eyes, they felt they had lost their youngest daughter, even though the loss wasn't one of physical demise.

Although Mum and Dad weren't socialising, they would attend church every Sunday. I would like to think that during their prayers, they would think of me and pray that I was doing all right. Although moving to Brisbane meant they had left all their friends behind, they had plenty of horiani living in Brisbane. They slowly started visiting some of these people, including their *simbetheri* (these are the parents of their son-in-laws). When two people marry, the respective parents of the couple are known to each other as simbetheri. This extends to the siblings of each one of the couple. This is the term they use to address one another. These visits were a start of some sort of normality, but they were nowhere near ready to go back to socialising like they did prior to me leaving the family. They were a long way off, being able to welcome people to their home like they used to and celebrate name days, Easter and Christmas. It was a sad, lonely existence for them, but they would try to cheer up when the grandchildren would visit. In my many phone calls to my sisters, they would let me know how Mum and Dad were going and they would tell me about how important it was for their grandchildren to be around them. I was saddened when I heard they weren't doing well, but hoped that in the future, this would change.

After living with my sister for six months, Mum and Dad bought their own home in Carina Heights, five minutes down the road from where they were living. They stayed close by to my sisters so they could help with the grandchildren. It was good for them to keep busy and not think about the situation they found themselves in, and especially not think about me.

During this first year, communication between us ceased entirely. I had no communication with my parents. How had my life come to this? This was not the future I envisaged for myself. I never wanted to have a lonely life without my family. My parents had now disowned me. The notion that my parents had disowned me gnawed at my heart. The weight of loneliness weighed heavily on me, a stark contrast to the life I had once imagined, surrounded by family.

The Fallout

Although my Mum could not read or write English, she addressed an envelope to me at my sister's address in Adelaide. Inside the envelope, I found a torn photograph of us taken on my 18th birthday, featuring my Mum, Dad, my sister, and me. Alongside the image, a small note in Greek was penned by my mother's hand, which read, "There will be no more happy times like this again." I knew she had written this as I recognised her handwriting. I was devastated. It was things like this that brought it all back and I cried for days.

When my parents disowned me and turned their backs on me, I could have done the same and turned my back on them. How I wished I could have. There were moments when their actions filled me with resentment and frustration, yet deep down, an enduring love for them persisted. Although I grappled with this internal struggle, my love for my parents remained steadfast. While this sentiment made perfect sense to me, I recognised it might seem strange to others, especially my non-Greek or non-Cypriot friends. Their inability to comprehend my unwavering love for my parents, who had rejected me, was a stark contrast to my own conviction. The cultural ties and the bond between my parents and I were at the heart of my feelings. I was feeling a mix of sadness and heartache.

The year ahead was a hard year for me. I went through some dark times but my love for my family made me push through this hardship and I was determined to make them accept me back into the family again. Whether this was going to take months, years, or decades, I was adamant that this would happen. It took me a while to let go of the guilt of having forced Mum and Dad away from Adelaide.

Soon after Mum and Dad left for Brisbane, I continued living with Mick and Louisa. I was determined that I wasn't going to 'live in sin'. This was something that was instilled in me from a young age, and I wanted to stick to this value. My relationship with Tony went from strength to strength. Tony was such a great support in those first few months when I was struggling to adjust to life without Mum and Dad. He was always there providing me with a lot of comfort and help during that time.

Mum and Dad moved to Brisbane in the October 1982 and as the calendar marked firsts without them it was getting more and more difficult. The first of these special occasions was Christmas Day. As I have explained earlier, all our celebrations were full of family, friends, and food. Given the circumstances, I spent Christmas Day with Tony's family as he was still not welcome at Mick and Louisa's place. I didn't want to spend Christmas apart from Tony. I always loved spending time with Tony's family. It gave me a sense of belonging now that I wasn't a part of my family like before.

Subsequently, when February rolled around, it was my first birthday without Mum and Dad. Traditionally, I would blow out the candles on my birthday cake with Mum, a sweet tradition that was shared by us as her birthday was two weeks later. Missing all the Greek Easter festivities was also very hard and not being able to celebrate Mum on Mother's Day, Dad on his birthday and then Father's Day also proved difficult. This created a void. Although I did not hear from them, I tried to stay connected. I would send Mother's Day and Father's Day cards to them, along with birthday cards on their special day. These still did not invoke any communication from them.

Throughout this first year, my emotions often spilled over into tears, making it even more challenging. Nonetheless, in the midst of these emotional tribulations, I was fortunate to have Tony by my side, offering his unwavering support and a comforting presence during those times of heartache.

Tony and I started doing things other normal couples did, going out for dinners, going to the movies and not having to hide from anyone. We started enjoying a newfound freedom. I remember going to the pictures, as we called it, and the drive-in to see movies like Flying High and Police Academy. I was now also able

The Fallout

to go out with my friends without having to ask permission. I remember going to the movies with Cathy to watch An Officer and a Gentleman.

As Mick was still determined that out of respect for my parents that Tony was still not allowed to come to the house, I would spend a lot of Saturday nights with Tony going to his sisters' places for dinner. We spent a lot of time with Netty and Ron, Tony's sister and brother-in-law.

Tony's dad and his stepmother offered for us to have an engagement party at their house. I was in two minds about having one as most of my family wouldn't be there, but I decided it was time to celebrate us. We had a lovely small gathering in the backyard at my father-in-law's with all of Tony's family, Cathy, Jack, Sophie and Desi.

Since I didn't have my own car, Tony would swing by to pick me up and we would go out and enjoy ourselves. He would always ensure I was back before my curfew. However, as time went on, my rebellious spirit began to push the boundaries once again, and I found myself coming home well past my curfew. Looking back, it's amazing to compare my experience with that of most 20-year-olds now, who enjoy the freedom of their own choices without curfew constraints. As I kept getting home later and later, it got to where Mick and I were clashing. I can't recall whether Mick asked me to leave or whether I decided it was time for a change, but moving out seemed to be the next step. Things couldn't stay the way they were; something needed to shift.

Leaving behind the comfort of my familiar surroundings, I was feeling anxious. It was yet another step into the unknown. I knew that the existing arrangement was no longer aligned with what I wanted. And so, with a mix of emotions and the promise of new experiences, I embarked on the next chapter of my life — a chapter that would pave the way for greater independence.

Tony wanting to show his commitment to me wanted me to move in with him. However, I remained hesitant about taking this significant step. Instead, I made the choice to move in with Tony's niece and her husband, a young couple who had recently married. This arrangement provided a bridge between Tony's wish and my own reservations, offering a compromise that allowed me to maintain a separate living space while still being closely connected to him. Tony spent quite a bit of time with me at his niece's house and it wasn't until they were expecting their first child that we all decided it was time for me to move out. It was collectively agreed that the timing was right for me to find a new place to live.

Just before moving out, I had been experiencing persistent pain in my abdomen. Initially, we thought it might have been appendicitis. However, after a trip to the doctor, an ultrasound and a specialist appointment, it was determined that a rather large cyst had developed on my ovary. The specialist compared it to the size of a dinner plate. This ovarian cyst, a fluid-filled sac, caused me considerable discomfort. Although I was told that they were common and almost every female would have one at some stage of their life, this didn't calm my anxiety over this situation. Although most cysts today are removed from ovaries by key-hole surgery, at the time I had to have the conventional open surgery. Because of this, my surgeon told me I would need six weeks off work to recuperate and I wasn't to lift anything heavy and driving a car was prohibited.

My sister Louisa wanted me to move back in with her temporarily so she could help take care of me. I asked her again if Tony would be welcome to their home as I wouldn't be able to go out right after the surgery. Sadly, Mick still said no to that idea. Tony and I talked it over and decided that I would move in with him. This seemed like the best choice for both of us.

At 20 years old, here I was, facing a situation I had never experienced before. I had never been to hospital, and interestingly, I hadn't even

The Fallout

been born in a hospital. Yet, I found myself with an ovarian cyst that required major surgery. It's in moments like these that a girl truly longs for the comforting presence of her mother. I'm uncertain about who exactly informed my parents about my surgery, but as soon as my dad got wind of it, he wanted to return to Adelaide to take care of me. However, my mother was adamant about not allowing him to do so.

I later came to know that visitors from Adelaide had visited my parents. It was during this visit that my dad's emotions came to the forefront. As the visitors were leaving, my dad stood outside, leaning on the car, his eyes welled up with tears. He asked them a question,

"Do you see my daughter? Do you see her at all?"

Their response was disheartening,

"No, we don't see her. We haven't seen her since you left Adelaide."

His voice was full of emotion, and my dad said to them,

"I heard she is having an operation and I want to go, but my wife won't let me."

Later, my sisters confirmed the extent of Dad's distress. He was deeply troubled, yearning to be by my side, especially because he knew this was my first experience with going to hospital and having an operation. He repeatedly expressed to them,

"My baby is having an operation. She will be all by herself. I want to be with her."

Although it seemed my Dad always had been the man of the house, this situation sure showed who was the boss. Mum forbade Dad from making the journey to Adelaide to be with me.

I moved into Tony's flat at Henley Beach. We tried to keep it as secretive as we could, as I still didn't want to disappoint my parents and have them find out I was living with Tony. I prepared for my surgery, asking work for six weeks off. They were very understanding and brought a temp in to help Cathy until I recovered. I had my surgery and convalesced at home. The added stress was waiting for the results to see whether the cyst was benign or malignant. Thankfully, the results came back negative; my cyst was benign. Tony looked after me until I was well enough to return to work. It was difficult not being able to go to Louisa's as I wasn't able to drive for six weeks, but she came and visited me and we spoke on the phone every day. It was quite daunting going through something like this without my mum by my side, but Cathy was a godsend and would come and sit with me when Tony was on the night shift.

Chapter Ten

The Hope and The Planning

*Loved you yesterday, love you still,
always have, always will - Elaine Davis*

Soon after my operation and when I was well enough, Tony and I started planning our future. We had a wedding to plan, invitations to send out, and decisions to make. Tony knew how important it was to me to get married in a Greek Orthodox Church, so he agreed, without hesitation.

Together, we visited the Greek Orthodox Church at Unley in South Australia, to meet with the priest. During our meeting, we explained our circumstances, particularly the fact that Tony had been divorced. The priest asked about Tony's baptismal status, to which he responded he had been christened in the Catholic church. At that moment, a fleeting thought crossed our minds – the possibility that Tony might need to be christened in the Greek church. How would that work? We wondered. Perhaps he would need to stand in a large bath of water and be immersed in water. However, since Tony was already christened as a Christian, he was exempt from this requirement and didn't need to convert his religion. I'm certain that if it had been necessary, Tony would have willingly changed religion for the sake of marrying in the Greek church, knowing how important it was to me.

One stipulation was that as we were getting married in the Greek church, our best man who was to exchange our rings and our stefana had to be Greek Orthodox. Tony had no hesitation in asking my godbrother, Jack to stand by his side as his best man. The first couple of decisions were made; we would get married in the Greek Orthodox church and Jack would be Tony's best man.

My choice of maid of honour was a simple decision to make. Cathy agreed to stand by my side. Together, we went dress shopping and did all the things brides and bridesmaids did together. As I was still in communication with my sisters, I checked with Mary if she was planning to make the trip to Adelaide to attend our wedding. As Mary said yes, I asked her daughter, my niece Marey, to be my flower girl. Mary was a dressmaker, and she agreed to make the flower-girl dress. When Mum would visit Mary, the dress would be hanging up in plain view. Mum would ask who that was for, prompting Mary to respond simply,

"It's for Dora's wedding."

The conversation would often stop there. My sisters didn't discuss the wedding or their impending attendance with my parents.

Cathy and I organised most of the wedding plans. I would also ring my sisters in Brisbane and ask their opinions on my colour scheme and other details. Tony and I chose our wedding invitations

The Hope and The Planning

and got them off to the printers. We also made our choice for the photographer that would capture our special day. Everything seemed to be falling into place.

As I intended on having a traditional Greek wedding, this also included Greek dancing at the reception. The only problem was Tony, Cathy and some of our friends didn't know how to Greek dance. It was then we decided that as part of our wedding preparations, we would meet once a week at our friends' house for me to teach them all the moves of our traditional Greek dances. They all wanted to learn so they could join in the festivities. My bond with these friends had grown remarkably strong, and we became quite close. They knew the difficulties I was having with Mum and Dad accepting Tony and as I didn't know whether my Dad would come to the wedding, walk me down the aisle and give me away, I asked my friend if he would be my "back-up" if Dad didn't come. He said he would be honoured. These nights spent learning Greek dances together turned into lots of enjoyment and we made cherished memories that would last forever.

Six weeks out from the wedding, it was time to send out our wedding invites. Another Cypriot tradition was that you would hand deliver as many of the invitations as you could, obviously posting the ones that were interstate or overseas. I did the right thing and sent an invitation to my parents, but with no response.

Still trying to be the dutiful daughter, I extended invitations to friends of my parents, who would have undoubtedly been on the guest list had my parents arranged the wedding like they did for all my other sisters. We didn't have the big wedding my sisters had, although it may be seen as big in other people's eyes. As Tony and I were paying for our own wedding, we kept it as low-key as we could without taking away from the dream that I always wanted a Big Greek Wedding. Our guest list included 120 family and friends.

As we started hand delivering our invitations, we got different reactions from people. My Thea Tsappou's place was the first stop on our list. I went and introduced Tony to Thea and Theo and gave them our wedding invitation. Thea invited us in and asked us to stay for lunch. She was just a beautiful soul, just accepting of us no matter what. When we went to one of my dad's koumbaro's house to deliver an invitation, his wife came to the door and she shuffled us into the lounge room. She offered us coffee, and it seemed like she kept us there away from her husband, as he was not interested in meeting with us at all. You can't please everyone and the truth be known, we didn't care if they accepted the invitation or not.

Here we were four weeks out from the wedding. I knew that some of my sisters were making the trip to Adelaide for my wedding and bringing their children. My sister Liz's husband Terry was also coming. This one particular day, I rang my sister to have a chat about the wedding plans and their trip down. Again, there were no mobiles then, so I rang the house phone. My sister wasn't home, but my then brother-in-law Terry was home. Terry answered the phone, and we chatted for a while when he said,

"Have you thought about coming to Brisbane?"

"What do you mean?" I asked.

He said, "Come to Brisbane and ask your mum and dad in person to come to the wedding. Ask your dad if he will give you away."

I couldn't believe what I was hearing, so I asked again, "What do you mean? I'm four weeks out from my wedding. They'll say to me, good, you're here now, you might as well stay."

Terry then explained how upset Dad was when I was in hospital, and he said to me,

"I really think it would mean a lot to them if you came up and invited them personally."

I said to him, "I don't think I can. I'm not sure what you're asking me."

Terry said, "Just come. Come and say to your mum and dad this is happening, I am marrying this man, I want you there."

I said, "Well, I'll talk to Tony, but I don't think so. I don't think he'd be happy with that, not that."

We went through so much heartache when my parents took me to Brisbane the last time. It was a real possibility that they wouldn't let me return, so we were both wary. Terry believed that if I came, this would be a major breakthrough if I wanted to reconnect with my parents. After the year I had, seeing family was so important as I wanted to feel that family connection again, but I still wasn't sure if I wanted to do this so close to the wedding.

Terry then said,

"I will guarantee that I will pick you up from the airport. I will take you to your mum and dad's house. You can sit and chat with them and however it goes, the minute it gets ugly, the minute they say you're staying here now, whatever is said I'll just put you back in the car, take you to the airport, and you're gone." Terry continued, saying, "At least then we know you tried."

I said, "I'll have to talk to Tony. I don't know." I couldn't give Terry an answer straight away.

That night, I talked to Tony, and he wasn't keen. I said,

"If there is a chance for them to be at our wedding, I would like that."

I was still confused. All these thoughts were going through my mind, but I finally decided to go to Brisbane and tell my parents that I loved them and to invite them personally to my wedding and ask my dad to give me away. And so the plan was put in place for me to go to Brisbane. I was only prepared to go for the weekend. I couldn't commit to any longer as I didn't want to put Tony through waiting for me again, wondering whether I would come back.

Tony dropped me at the airport and I was feeling very anxious, apprehensive and every other feeling that made me sick in the stomach. However, I had made my decision to give this a try. At least then I could say I did all in my power to ensure Mum and Dad were at my wedding and that my dad walked me down the aisle. Terry picked me up from the airport and took me to Mum and Dad's place. As I walked in their front door, I fought the urge to turn around and leave. I knew that reconnecting after being estranged for a year would be awkward.

When I walked in, they both hugged me. Dad was teary and was very warm towards me. Mum was a little sarcastic towards me. I didn't know how to react; I didn't know what to feel. We engaged in small talk, exchanging pleasantries and asking about each other's health. Dad then asked if I was happy and whether I was still planning on going ahead with the wedding.

"Yes," I said. "I am happy and I am marrying Tony."

I kept telling them I loved them, they kept saying If you did you wouldn't be doing this to us, and I said,

"Well, I do love you and I am going to get married, and I'd love for you to be there."

Dad asked me a poignant question. He looked at me with his sad eyes and he said,

"Who's going to give you away?" My immediate response was, "Of course I want you to. I want you to give me away."

"And if I don't?" he said.

"I'll worry about that then, but I really would love for you to give me away. Would you do this for me *baba*?"

Dad couldn't give me an answer. They didn't give me an indication if they would come. After a few hours, I said goodnight and told them I was staying at Liz's for the weekend. I promised Mum and Dad I would be back in the morning to say goodbye before I left for the airport. I left that night from Mum and Dad's place thinking that sometimes we have to go outside our comfort zone if we want results.

The next day, as the good Greek daughter, I went by and said my goodbyes, still not knowing whether they would make the trip for my wedding. I left, not knowing whether I would see them again. Not knowing whether they would ever talk to me again. This goodbye was the hardest I had ever had to say. They had a big decision to make, and I knew I would be anxiously awaiting their response. They gave me no indication of what their decision would be. My eyes welled as I kissed my parents goodbye. I went back to Adelaide and continued on with our plans.

A couple of weeks before the wedding, I got word that Mum and Dad had decided to come to the wedding. I received this news with mixed emotions. What would this mean? Would they be happy for me? Would they smile at my wedding? I was getting very excited that the wedding was getting closer and even more excited to see my family again. As each of my family members arrived, the excitement grew even more. I gave them all the biggest hugs I had ever given them. So happy that they had brought Mum and Dad with them. As a lead up to the wedding, it was good seeing my parents reconnecting with their friends and a little smile returning to their faces. Although I knew it would be small baby steps, I could see that maybe there was a light at the end of the tunnel. Maybe what I had gone through this last year was worth it. I could see myself being accepted back into the family fold. Something I was working so hard towards. Tony was also excited for me, as he knew how much it meant for me to have my family by my side at our wedding. How I would have loved to have all my family at my wedding but unfortunately that wasn't to be, but I was happy for those who would be celebrating with me. Although it was early days, the thought of having my parents back in my life felt wonderful. Everything I had dreamt of.

Louisa had them all stay at her place. It was again, like old times when everybody would stay at my mum and dad's when my sisters would visit. The Saturday afternoon before the wedding, Louisa hosted a kitchen tea for me at her place. My sisters and aunties helped out making treats for the guests. There was a combination of the old favourites: curried eggs, cheese triangles, pavlova and Greek sweets. Everyone came and enjoyed a lovely afternoon tea and came bearing gifts. When the kitchen tea was over, Tony came over to transport the gifts to his place, where we would be setting up home.

My dad asked Tony to go outside for a chat.

"Oh dear," I thought.

"What's this about?"

Dad started talking slowly and considered his every word.

"When you marry Dora, I don't want you to call me Andrew. I know someone who calls his father-in-law by his first name. I don't like that."

"What would you like me to call you?" Tony asked.

"My five other son-in-laws call me Dad and that's what I would like you to call me too."

The Hope and The Planning

"I'd be honoured," said Tony.

And that was that. From that day forward, Tony called him Dad, and he called my mum, Mum. I was so happy. Tony says that the day Dad asked him to call him Dad was a defining moment for him. If he hadn't asked Tony to do that, Tony said he would have felt that he was simply my Dad but when he asked him to call him Dad, that suited him entirely. That changed everything for him. Although it was only early days, Tony finally felt that he was part of the family.

The week leading up to the wedding, us girls got together and carried on the tradition of helping Cathy make the bonbonniere. My life seemed like it was slowly going back to some normality.

Chapter Eleven

Open Arms

*There is only one happiness in this life,
to love and be loved - George Sand*

Finally, the day arrived; every bride dreams of the perfect day. There are always nerves, but my feelings were a little different from just the usual wedding day nerves. It is one thing to hope that all the details go without a hitch, but I was worried about how Mum and Dad would be at my wedding. Would they be sad all day? Would they make a scene?

The day started as a normal day for any bride. Hair and makeup. My sisters and Cathy helped me get dressed. I certainly needed it as my wedding dress had a full hoop petticoat which I needed help to get into. Our wedding day was a vision of timeless elegance. I always dreamt of getting married in a grand white dress like the ones seen in the classic movie 'Gone with the Wind'. I always thought this style looked so romantic. And so, my dress was made of white lace, with a high neck, and a hooped petticoat underneath, which gave it an elegant fullness and had a vintage charm about it. My dress flowed gracefully and my long veil trailed behind me. I held a beautiful bouquet that featured white and burgundy carnations. The same type of carnation Tony wore pinned to his lapel on the deep blue suit he wore.

Cathy stood by my side, taking on the role of both maid of honour and bridesmaid. Her dress was a rich burgundy with a hooped petticoat. The cream lacework added a touch of vintage charm, and I chose a parasol for her to hold rather than a bouquet. My adorable flower girl, Marey looked like a princess in her lace-covered dress, much like mine and Cathy's. Marey's dress was also enhanced with a hooped petticoat and she too held a white parasol. This all transformed our special day into the cherished memories we now have.

Leading up to my wedding day, there were thoughts going around in my head about whether Mum and Dad would want to carry out the Cypriot traditions. I was very grateful to hear that they did. My family and friends gathered at my sister's house. First, my dad tied the red zoni around my waist. Mum then burned the incense and dried olive leaves in the kabnistiri. Dad accompanied me in the old classic black Daimler Tony had organised for us to make the trip to the St Spyridon Greek Orthodox church at Unley. As I only had a small bridal party, Cathy and Marey also accompanied us in the car.

Looking back at my wedding photos, I can see that Dad was not the happiest he could have been, but he was there. It was a start. In the Greek church, we don't have an organ playing or a song playing. Dad just simply walked me down the aisle. He took me to the altar and lifted my veil. How hard it would have been to 'give me away' to a man he was still not convinced was the best person for me. Right from the start, Tony and I went into our relationship with the motto, 'We'll show everyone our union was the right thing.' Throughout the next 40 years, we stuck by this.

My flower girl and page boy stood up at the altar holding the white candles. Our service was mainly in Greek with some English. Guests told me later that they couldn't understand the English because of the priest's strong Greek accent. I had anticipated that this might be the case and had the service printed in English in booklets that were given out to the guests on arrival. The priest took our rings and made the sign of the cross on our foreheads. The rings were then placed on our fingers on our right hands. Jack stepped forward and changed the rings three times. Cathy then stepped forward and changed the rings. The priest then crowned us with our stefana which were connected to each other with a silk ribbon that symbolised unity.

The maid of honour is also referred to as koumbara in the Greek Church. When we met with the priest, and he told us that our best man had to be Greek Orthodox, I asked whether Cathy of Italian descent and christened Catholic could be my koumbara. The priest explained that there was no reason she couldn't stand at the altar by my side. She was allowed to exchange our rings but as she was not Greek Orthodox, she could not exchange our stefana. On our wedding day, when it was time to exchange the stefana, this little detail got overlooked, and the priest guided Cathy to come forward and exchange them after Jack had finished. Nobody wanted to point out that the priest had made a mistake, so Cathy also got to exchange the stefana and this further sealed a bond between the three of us.

The time came during the ceremony when the priest offered us wine from the beautiful chalice that they use in the Greek church. This holds a deep symbolism yet the funny part of this was that it was us that provided the port for this part of the ceremony. I remember Tony specifically saying we only get three sips so let's buy the cheapest bottle of wine we can find. What a wrong choice we made. It was a very hot day, and we had been going all day. The thought of something wet to quench our parched throats was appealing. We each took a sip and our faces said it all. It was far from nice; actually, it was disgusting, the taste was awful. We forced down the two more sips and the ceremony continued. At the end of that part of the ceremony the priest, takes the chalice and finishes the remaining wine. In that moment, all we could think of was the poor priest, who had to graciously consume the dreadful wine we'd chosen. We exchanged knowing glances and thought perhaps we should have invested a little more in this particular aspect of the ceremony. The priest then walked us around the altar three times, a symbolic ritual that spoke of his guidance into family life for us. We circled the altar with smiles on our faces. We loved that our ceremony was full of not only poignant moments but amusing ones that added to the richness of our story.

After the service concluded, our friends and family came to offer their well wishes and warm embraces. Following this gathering, we went to Bonython Park in Adelaide to capture the essence of our love in photographs. The gardens' backdrop provided the perfect canvas with one particular photo capturing us looking into the lake with our shadow in the water. We have some beautiful photos to remember our special day for eternity.

The day was far from over. It was now time to celebrate. As Tony and I had funded our wedding on our own, we had a much smaller wedding than my sisters. We had 120 guests and held our reception at the elegant setting of the Tower House at Beaumont. After dinner was served, it was time for speeches. The usual speeches came from Jack, Cathy and Tony. My father-in-law got up and said a few words. It was time for my dad's speech. At each of my sister's weddings, Dad gave a speech. I think his emotions came over him and he asked Terry if he would give the speech he had prepared. Terry gave a speech on my dad's behalf. It was very emotional. After we cut our cake, the moment we had dreamt of was finally here - our first dance as man and wife. We danced to our favourite song, Open Arms by Journey. In that moment, nothing else mattered, just the two of us looking into each other's eyes and thinking, we did it! We made it! We were now happily married and my parents were at the wedding. Our second dance was to Elvis Presley's Forever My Darling. It was during our second dance that the Cypriot tradition of pinning money onto our outfits as newlyweds occurred. Our wedding day wasn't just a union of two hearts; it was a mix of cultures, traditions, and stories. Each element created a memory that would last forever.

After the band invited the bridal party and our friends and family to the dance floor for a few more dances, they soon took a break and we put on a tape of Cypriot music and my bridal party got up and danced the traditional Cypriot dances I had taught them leading up to the wedding. Everyone then joined in and we had a wonderful night. It was soon time for us to bid our farewell. Our guests made a circle and Tony and I went around saying goodbye to every one of them. Saying goodbye to my sisters and my parents was very tearful, as I knew they would be heading back to Brisbane.

The very next day we headed to Brisbane for our honeymoon. Tony and I had a wonderful week at the Gold Coast, where we did all the tourist attractions and then we spent a week at my sister's house. After that week, my parents asked if we would consider extending our holiday and stay with them for a week. This would mean we would spend our first Christmas as a married couple in Brisbane. As we both had leave from work and didn't need to rush back to Adelaide, we agreed to stay. I rang Cathy and told her we wouldn't be home for Christmas and the only reason she was upset was that she had gifted us a small Christmas tree as our Christmas present.

"That's alright," I said, "we'll use it next year."

Little did we know that the very next Christmas we would have moved to Brisbane permanently.

Our first year of married life went by quickly. We loved going for walks along the beach before cooking dinner on the days Tony was on day shifts. The other days I would eat dinner alone, in front of the TV, something I hadn't done before, or I would ask Cathy to come and join me for dinner. One night Tony, Cathy and I were heading out for a night out but decided to have dinner at ours before we went out. I had made a Shepherd's Pie, so grateful about how it turned out, as it was my first time making it. It looked just like it did in the cookbook. I went to get it out of the oven and even though I had my kitchen gloves on, I must not have had a good grip on the casserole and the whole thing came crashing down. The look on my face said it all.

"It's ok," said Tony, trying to appease me.

"It's fine," said Cathy.

The next minute we all started laughing uncontrollably.

"Anyone for Pizza?" I asked, trying to make light of the situation. So, pizza it was.

In the February 1984, I turned 21. Tony told me we were going to his sister Netty's place for a quiet birthday dinner and that it would be just us. When I got there, they had organised a surprise 21st for me. I was so overwhelmed. They had invited my family and friends. My father-in-law and I celebrated our birthdays three days apart, so when it came time to blow out the candles, Netty brought out two cakes, one for my 21st and one for her dad. Netty had organised a lovely cake in the shape of the number 74. The only problem was she got it wrong, as Dad was only turning 73. She never lived that down. My father-in-law was quite a joker, and he kept ribbing her about this for many years to come. These were wonderful times we shared together.

During that first year, we were contemplating the prospect of relocating to Brisbane. We had such a wonderful time on our honeymoon and although we knew that you shouldn't rate what it would be like living and working in a different state when you were on holiday, we thought we could live in Brisbane. We loved the weather and Tony seemed to get on well with most of my family. Mum and Dad were accepting of our relationship now that we were married.

I had a heartfelt conversation with Tony, emphasising that the ultimate decision had to be his, as I never wanted to bear the burden of separating him from his children. The circumstances were starkly different then. Through no fault of his own, the courts granted full custody to Tony's ex-wife. These times were especially trying for Tony, as he faced significant obstacles in spending time with his kids. Notably, Children's Services had made it difficult for him to see his children, since his accommodation at the time had only one spare room instead of two, which was necessary for the children to have their own rooms during weekend visits. This situation prevented Tony from having the children stay with him and even simple visits proved to be an uphill battle. After much consideration and discussion, we decided to make the move to Brisbane. We gave ourselves a six-month window to carefully plan and prepare for this significant change in our lives. I recall during that challenging period Tony telling me,

"The children will come to me when they're ready."

His words carried a sense of patience and understanding, reflecting his unwavering love and commitment to his children's well-being. Tony's belief in the eventual reconnection with his kids, based on their own readiness, provided us with a glimmer of hope and strength as we embarked on our journey to Brisbane.

Soon after our first wedding anniversary, Tony had a disappointing setback at work when he was overlooked for a promotion. He came home from work and said,

"If you want to move to Brisbane, let's do it now."

"Why, what's happened?" I asked.

After telling me he missed out on the promotion, he said he wanted to throw his job in and move to Brisbane. I was feeling a whirlwind of emotions; happiness, joy, sadness, and elation. He looked at me, waiting for my response. It felt like he had just asked me to marry him all over again.

"Yes," I replied. "Yes, let's do it."

With that decision made, we started putting our plans in place. The hardest thing was telling Cathy. Although she was disappointed, she was happy for us.

We packed up our belongings and submitted our resignations. Even before leaving Adelaide, I actively began the process of job hunting in Brisbane. As Tony was using his long service leave, we decided he would have some time off and pick up some odd jobs painting houses, as he was a painter by trade. We sold what we could and packed the rest of our household goods in a truck and the rest of our personal belongings in my trusty little blue Torana. The story behind my little blue Torana is rather funny.

In Adelaide, when obtaining a driver's license, there was no requirement to choose between a manual or automatic transmission. I took my driving test in an automatic car, yet my license was issued as an open license. When Tony and I began the search for my first car, we both took a liking to a 1972 LJ Torana. I was drawn to its appearance and colour, while Tony, with his mechanical insight, said it was of sound condition. However, there was one hitch - it was a manual. I had never driven a manual car before.

"It'll be alright," said Tony. "I'll teach you."

Famous last words. So, I bought the car. We shared many laughs, and we both used some expletives while Tony taught me how to drive my new car. After lots of kangaroo hops, I finally mastered the art of driving a manual car.

So, we drove to Brisbane. Tony did most of the driving, only giving me the wheel once. We took our time as we weren't in a hurry, stopping overnight in a motel in West Wyalong and Tamworth. Whilst driving, I stopped at a phone box and rang Louisa to let her know how we were travelling. Louisa had a phone message for me to ring the University of Queensland Student Union for a job interview. I couldn't believe my luck. I quickly rummaged through my handbag for some more coins and rang the number I had scribbled down. By the time we took off for the rest of our trip, I had secured myself a job interview at the University of Queensland Union. How exciting!

We arrived in Brisbane a week before Christmas. Having made significant progress in mending our relationship with my parents, they were happy to have us stay with them until we found our feet. The day after we arrived, Tony took me to the St Lucia campus of the University of Queensland. By the time I got back home, they had rung me with a job offer. I was to begin in the new year as the Student Union's Executive Officer, directly working with the President and Secretary of the University of Queensland Union (UQU). Looking forward, a lot of the Student Union Executive I worked with then, now hold prominent positions in the Queensland Government, including some Ministers and the current Premier of Queensland. We had a lot of fun working there in the 80s.

Those first few months while I was going off to work, Tony was at home with Mum and Dad picking up odd painting jobs here and there. When I'd get home from work Mum would say,

"Tony doesn't like my food, does he?"

I would reassure Mum that he did like her food but that he was used to eating a sandwich for lunch, not a whole hot meal. I think she was trying to fatten him up, as he was very skinny when we first got married. So dutifully she would start making him sandwiches for lunch. As Tony was home through the day, one particular day I got home from work and we were going out for dinner. I asked Tony,

"While I have a shower, can you iron my dress?"

Mum was still of the view that men did not do chores like this. Tony would hide my dress under his arm and race downstairs to the laundry and iron it before Mum would see him. If Mum saw him, she would start on me,

"Why are you getting your husband to iron your dress for you? That's not a man's job."

There were a lot of adjustments when we first lived with Mum and Dad. We saved our money and bought a house of our own as soon as we could.

I loved working at UQU and it was only months into my first job in Brisbane that we found out I was pregnant. Those mixed feelings once again took over. Although Tony had his vasectomy reversed, we went into our marriage not knowing if we were going to be able to conceive, so although the timing wasn't great and it would mean I wouldn't be entitled to any paid maternity leave we were beyond excited. We weren't actively trying to start a family. When I was late with my period, I waited two weeks after the date it was due and made an appointment with my doctor. Back then, there weren't the tests available now where you could find out days after you became pregnant. We went in and the doctor said they would send away for the results and they would ring me when they were back. To our delight, the result was positive. We couldn't believe our luck. We knew that a lot of other people would wait until they were further along to announce to the world they were expecting, but we were both so excited we couldn't hold back. Everyone, including my parents, was so happy for us. This would be their thirteenth grandchild. Tony rang his Dad and the rest of his family in Adelaide and they too were excited for us. In my excitement, I started buying things the baby would need, little outfits, a blanket, a rattle. I devoted the bottom drawer of my chest of drawers as the 'baby's drawer'. My Mum would say to me,

"You know it's bad luck to buy things for the unborn child before their birth."

This was an old superstition.

"Oh Mum," I would say, "That's just an old wives' tale." And so, I continued buying little booties and singlets and putting them in the bottom drawer.

The first week rolled into the next and before I knew it I was eleven weeks pregnant. Not quite past my first trimester, but nearly there. This day Tony was at work and I was getting ready to leave for work when suddenly I felt a sensation down my leg. I called out to Mum,

"I'm bleeding."

Mum laid me down on the bed and rang one of my sisters. Without hesitation, my sister rushed me to the hospital where I was taken straight to emergency. I really didn't know what was happening. Nobody was providing any clear information. Meanwhile, Mum and Dad contacted Tony, and he made his way to the hospital. I could hear him at the nurses' station asking after me.

"We don't have anyone here with that name," they responded.

"I just received a call to say she was brought here."

Just as he was finishing his sentence, he saw me being wheeled into a ward. As soon as he saw me, we both started crying. Rather than placing us somewhere private, I was wheeled into a ward of mothers who had just had their babies and their babies were next to their beds in their little cribs. Still, I had no confirmation that I had had a miscarriage. Doctors and nurses were coming in and out of the ward, but not saying a word. It wasn't until they came to wheel me away to conduct a curettage procedure that we realised that I had suffered a miscarriage, losing my precious baby. Although I had been pregnant for only eleven weeks, in my heart, this was a baby I had cherished from the moment I received the news of my pregnancy.

I wish someone had told me it was ok to grieve my baby. The baby I didn't know whether I would be able to have. Everyone around me was trying to make me feel better, but they didn't understand that no matter what they said, I wasn't going to feel better, not today, not tomorrow, and not anytime soon. I felt like I couldn't go on and that I didn't want to continue living. Not that I had suicidal thoughts, but I just wasn't ready to continue with life as it was before I had the miscarriage. However, I had to find the strength from somewhere to carry on. I had one week off from work and the day I returned to work, I knew it was going to be hard. On my desk was a card from all the office staff saying, 'Thinking of You'. Everyone wrote, sorry for your loss. I know they were just trying to do the right thing. People were scared to ask me how I was. They didn't know what to say, and they didn't know how I would react. After I had been at work for about an hour one of the women from the office next door came and told me that they had a temp coming in to cover for the busy period and that she wanted to let me know before I bumped into her that she was pregnant. She was five months pregnant and showing, so she wanted to give me the heads up before I saw her.

At morning tea time I went into the staff room to make myself a cuppa and there in front of me was this temp. She introduced herself and said,

"The women have told me what you have just gone through and I am so sorry."

"It's ok," I replied.

"It's not your fault, it's not anyone's fault." We got talking, and we clicked straight away. We told each other about our story of falling in love and she too had a similar story as she was Italian and married an Australian. We became good friends.

Chapter Twelve

My Big Fat Happy Ending

*Life is too short. Grudges are a waste of happiness.
Laugh when you can, apologise when you should, and let
go of what you can't change.
Love deeply and forgive quickly. Life is too short to be
unhappy. – Author unknown*

One year after my miscarriage, we were on top of the world when it was confirmed I was pregnant again. This time, we agreed to keep it quiet for as long as we could. The only issue was I had morning sickness, morning, noon and night, so it was a little difficult to keep it under wraps.

In March 1987, I became a mother for the first time. People always say that having a baby brings a special kind of love, but you don't really understand it until it happens to you. The love we both had for our daughter, the daughter we didn't know whether we'd be able to have was just incredible. She was a precious gift. We named her after my mum, Myrofora in Greek, and Mia for short. Mia's full name is Mia Catherine, named after our koumbara Cathy. Tony had told me that having kids would bring my parents even closer to us, and he was right. Life was wonderful. It seemed perfect. I was living in Brisbane close to my sisters watching my nieces and nephews grow up together with my daughter and most importantly my parents were in my daughter's life. Life went on like this for years. I went back to work while Mia was quite young and my parents looked after her. Mia formed quite a close bond with her Yiayia and Pappou.

Mum and Dad looked after both our kids while I worked, which meant both Mia and Andrew spoke Greek before they spoke English. This forced Tony to learn Greek, and he actually spoke more Greek than he did Dutch. He even went to Greek lessons at night to get a better appreciation of the language. Tony has very much taken on the Greek culture. He's often heard saying, "They're not Greek like us."

Much happened in the years that followed. We had our ups and downs. Tony's children were teenagers now, and they both asked to come and holiday in Brisbane. We introduced them to their younger sister and their brother Andrew, who was born in 1991. We named Andrew after my dad, Andreas in Greek and Andrew in English. He was given my father-in-law's name as his middle name, John. We had lovely holidays together with all our kids at the Gold Coast, taking them to the theme parks and enjoying each other's company. Tony's children have also visited us many times since, as adults.

We now celebrated every major milestone, with my parents and all my family. Our children's birthdays, Mother's Day, Father's Day, Greek Easter and Christmas. We would all gather at Mum and Dad's house. Although the house was small, there was plenty of room in the backyard for us all to gather and enjoy our celebrations, even if it meant Pappou yelling at the kids for accidentally kicking the football into his garden. The cousins grew up like brothers and sisters. They were all great friends and loved spending time together. I used to worry about not being part of a big Cypriot family, but this certainly changed as I was a big part of everyone's life. We did everything together. We went on holidays together, to the Gold Coast, Sydney and Adelaide. We went on picnics together and spent many nights yelling at the TV when the NRL State of Origin was on. These are all wonderful memories we now have.

When Christmas would come around, I made sure that it was the most magical time for our kids. Even as adults now, I still tell them,

"Stop believing and you'll stop receiving."

Each year I hang a Christmas stocking for my adult children as well as my grandchildren, and I love seeing that big smile on their faces on Christmas morning.

Over the next few years, we would experience much sadness. Six months after Mia was born, we got word from Adelaide that my father-in-law passed away. As flights were so expensive back then and I had Mia as a six-month-old, Tony made a trip back to Adelaide alone to bury his father. Years later, we also had other sad news with the death of my brother-in-law Ron, our nephew Mark and Tony's stepmother. Tony's ex-wife also passed away and Tony flew down to be with his kids for the funeral. A great sadness came over us when my eldest sister Helen passed away. She had battled breast cancer, which eventually moved to her bones. Helen lost her battle in 1997. The whole family was by her side when she took her last breath.

This was a very sad time in our lives and it affected Mum and Dad deeply. No parent should have to bury their child. This time, Mum and Dad really were in mourning. Mum donned her black attire and did not take it off until she herself died many years later. This was a very dark time for my parents but although they were very sad, whenever their grandchildren came to visit, they made sure they would smile. Each of the grandchildren, no matter which one in the pecking order, would put a smile on Mum and Dad's faces as well. Mum and Dad had 17 grandchildren and were lucky enough to meet eight of their great-grandchildren. Losing Helen felt like a piece of the puzzle from our family was missing. My sisters and I wore black for the first twelve months after she died. This was a mark of respect to Helen but also to my mum and dad. Another tradition we all adhered to.

Tony and I went through quite a bit over the years. It seemed like every time Christmas was approaching, something major would happen to Tony. One year, three days before Christmas, Tony had a triple bypass. The doctors said that he would need to be in the ICU for five days and the children weren't allowed in the ICU. Tony was very young when he went through his major surgery and, because of his wit and determination, he got out of the ICU within three days. This meant I could bring our children to visit him on Christmas day. It was a long road to recovery. He had to convalesce at home for three months. But we got through it. You will recall Tony did not have to change religion to marry me in the Greek Orthodox Church. Having faced this near-death experience, Tony asked my father what steps would be needed for him to be christened in the Greek Orthodox church. Consequently, he was christened in the Greek church in Brisbane, a testament to the deep love and commitment that bound us together. My father chose a lovely family friend to be his godmother. As Tony was already christened Catholic, he wasn't required to have the full christening with a deep-water baptism, but simply needed to follow some of the other Greek Orthodox traditions, including the cutting of a lock of his hair. For those who know Tony, he had hair back then.

A few years later, again around Christmas, Tony had an accident at work and had an injury to his eye. He ended up having a corneal transplant. Luckily, it all went well as we have been told people can reject organ transplants. Along with these difficult times, we had some wonderful, happy times. Our first granddaughter, Tiarnah was born in 2006. Although she lived with her mum in Adelaide, they would come and spend Christmas with us each year. We love her dearly and although I am not her blood, she calls me Yiayia and she is nothing but my granddaughter.

Over the next 20 or 30 years, my sisters and their husbands started drifting apart. We can't definitely say that arranged marriages aren't successful, considering my parents were married for over 65 years, and Andy and Angie are approaching their 52nd wedding anniversary. However, among the six of us sisters, only Angie and her husband, along with Tony and myself, remain married. Similar to all aspects of life, generalizations fall short. Arranged marriages succeed in certain cases, but others, (just like many individuals who marry for love) end in divorce.

As there were only two sons-in-law still in the family, Tony was called on by Mum and Dad whenever they needed something. Ironically, this forbidden son-in-law was now the one running to their aid when their TV stopped working, when they needed something painted, or when at election time, we would bundle Mum and Dad up in the car and take them with us to the polling booths to vote.

I was definitely the black sheep of the family, but my actions were the catalyst for opening up my parents' eyes and being able to accept things they would not have been able to accept before I married Tony.

Some members of my family had children out of wedlock, something many years ago, my parents would not have been able to accept. We also started welcoming people from different origins into our family. Although my parents didn't make it to see my daughter Mia get married, they loved her choice of partner. Paul is Samoan. Mum and Dad welcomed all these family members to their home. My Dad would often say to my son-in-law,

"When are you going to marry my granddaughter? You need to hurry up if I'm going to witness this before I die."

Unfortunately, he didn't make it to their wedding, but he was happy for them to be together. Our first daughter Sally got married in 2013, followed by Mia and Paul in 2014. We had the most beautiful weddings for both of them.

My parents were still alive and got to meet our granddaughter Tiarnah and accepted her as one of their own. Mia and Paul have also given us two grandchildren, Harlan and Nylah, and I know how much my parents would have loved them. My grandchildren know all about big Pappou and big Yiayia and following our Greek Orthodox faith, speak of them being up in heaven and talk about them often. Ironically, another funny story relating to my birth at home is that 56 years later, I delivered my granddaughter Nylah in a car because my daughter Mia didn't make it to the hospital.

Over the years, I found myself in a similar situation to my mum and dad where Tony and I opened up our home for friends and family to come and live with us when they moved to Brisbane or were moving house. We had one sister with her husband and two kids live with us for 18 months. Tony's son came and lived with us. My nieces and nephews were also welcomed into our home, as was our dear friend Sophie from Adelaide. As Mum and Dad got older, a lot of our Christmas and other festivities were held at our place. We had many New Year's Eve parties altogether to bring in the new year. It's nice to now see my daughter and nieces taking over this role. Life really is about spending time with the ones you love. I couldn't imagine my life without my family. Life really takes full circle.

Both Tony and I have always had a community spirit about us. Over the years, I organised many successful events raising money for Breast Cancer because of the untimely death of my sister Helen from the disease. When Louisa was also diagnosed with Breast

Cancer, this charity pulled at my heartstrings further. Together with my sisters, nieces, Tony and my brother-in-law Andy, we raised much-needed funds for this worthy cause. To add to the community work, Tony became a Justice of the Peace and, whilst he was working, would always see people after hours to witness documents when needed. Now that he has retired, he has joined the JPs in Community and serves a couple of times a month at the shopping centres.

As the years went by, my elderly parents' health started declining. In 2010, Mum was officially diagnosed with dementia. Whilst Dad was sick himself, he ended up being Mum's full-time carer. This was quite a difficult time, as Dad couldn't understand what dementia was. He couldn't understand the changes that were happening to Mum. Why couldn't she understand him? Why couldn't she look after herself? Dad would often lie on his bed and say to me,

"I'm not well. What's going to happen to your mother? What's going to happen when I'm gone? Who's going to look after your mum?"

Angie and I both promised him we would look after Mum. Trying to put his mind at ease, we asked him to concentrate on his own health and not to worry about things like that. We made him a promise that we would be by her side. In May 2012, my dad passed away. His death hit us all very hard, especially the grandkids. Six of his grandsons carried his casket to his grave. The grandchildren all put a beautiful eulogy together to honour their Pappou.

After Dad died, Tony and I first moved in with Mum to keep her in her familiar surroundings and to look after her. Mum was at the stage where she could not live independently. She could not look after herself. My sister Angie and I were determined to keep the promise we made to Dad to take care of our mum. Since Angie wasn't working, we decided she would stay with Mum during the day while I kept working. When I finished work, I'd go home to take over from Angie, making sure Mum was fed, cared for, and put to bed. Mum would wake up several times during the night. Some of those nights, Tony would nudge me and tell me that Mum was either tickling his feet or trying to climb into bed with us. After eight long months of juggling full-time work and around-the-clock care for Mum, it was decided that Andy and Angie would take over from us and move in to look after Mum. Angie was Mum's primary carer during the week and Tony and I would care for her on the weekends at our place. These times were very tough for all of us. Taking care of Mum while she was living with dementia was the most challenging thing I've ever done. I wouldn't change it for the world. I never regretted one minute of it. We did our best to make Mum comfortable in her last months of life. Andy and Angie stayed living with Mum until she passed away in December 2013. This too hit the family very hard and the grandchildren once again were devastated.

My sisters and I have kept the traditions going. We go to church and the cemetery, lighting a candle on each anniversary of my parents' deaths. We held a *mnimosino* (memorial) after 40 days from the time of their death, three months, six months, nine months, and now each anniversary of their death. We keep a candle burning in our homes to keep their memory eternal.

As I reflect on my life, I realise that life's journey can be full of surprises. The man who was once seen as a xeno, an outsider to our family, a stranger, turned out to be the strongest source of support for my parents as they grew older. The differences and problems that initially caused issues between him and our family were slowly overcome by the passing years. They were replaced by strong connections built through shared experiences and responsibilities. In the final chapter of my parents' lives, along with Andy and Angie, it was me; the disowned daughter and the once forbidden son-in-law Tony who stood by their side. Tony helped me tend to their needs and cared for my mother like she was his own. It was he who provided comfort and solace to not only them but me in the last years of their lives. This is a poignant reminder that love, in all its forms, has the power to heal wounds and rewrite destinies. The most beautiful stories are often the ones that defy expectations, reminding us that forgiveness can light the way even in the darkest of times.

Over the last few years, Tony and I have decided that you never know when your time is up, so we have been enjoying life to the maximum. We have travelled. We have been to destinations like Bali, Vietnam and Europe with my niece Anthea and her husband Harry. We have explored the vibrant cultures of these countries and enjoyed the markets and street food. Our European journey was filled with iconic landmarks and charming cities, where we created cherished memories. We had a wonderful time immersing ourselves in the rich history of these places. It is so wonderful to share these experiences in the company of loved ones.

We have also been to Hawaii, New Zealand, the UK, The Netherlands, Cyprus, and Greece with other members of our family. Just this last year we took the grandchildren to Disneyland in California where we made more wonderful memories. We also saw some other parts of the United States, including Wisconsin, where we met Tony's cousins that he had never met before. We have enjoyed all these travels, but two special places in both our hearts were Cyprus, where my parents were born and the Netherlands where Tony was born.

I have certainly ticked quite a few things off my bucket list, including visiting Graceland where Elvis Presley is buried. And now I can tick another thing off my bucket list and that is that I am a published author. Who would have thought? Dreams do come true.

And my final thought is, as it turned out, I really was a Good Little Greek Girl, just not quite the type my parents would have wanted me to be.

> *The freedom to be yourself is a gift only you can give yourself. But once you do, no one can take it away*
> *— Doe Zantamata*

GLOSSARY

Avgolemoni	Egg and Lemon Soup
Baba	Dad
Baklava	Greek sweet
Baoulo	Glory box
Bonbonniere	A keepsake for guests to take home from a christening or wedding
Briki	Small pot to make Greek Coffee
Calamari	Octopus
Catsarola	Cooking Pot of food
Christos Anesti	Christ has risen
Cotoletta	Italian Schnitzel
Dolmathes	Stuffed Vine leaves
Galaktoboureko	Custard pie
Gliko	A sweet of fruit cooked in syrup
Halloumi	Cypriot cheese
Horiani	People from the same village

Kabnistiri	A vessel to burn incense
Kai Sta Thika Sou	And to yours
Kaimaki	Film on top of a Greek Coffee
Keftethes	Meatballs
Kokkinisto	A dish of lamb, potatoes and cauliflower marinated in port wine
Komboloi	Worry Beads
Koufeta	The making of the bonbonniere
Koumbara	Maid of Honour and/or Godmother to your child
Koumbaro	Best Man/Godfather to your child
Krevati	Bed – a celebration for the preparation of the marital bed
Logo	Word – a commitment ceremony
Loucoumades	Honey Puffs
Mezethes	Snacks
Mira	Celebration held 3 days after a christening
Mnimosino	Memorial
Nifi	Bride, daughter-in-law, wife
Nouna	Godmother
Paploma	Mattress – a celebration for the preparation of the marital bed
Pappou	Grandfather
Pastitio	Greek macaroni and meat pie (like a lasagna)
Proxenio	Arranged marriages
Proxenitis	Matchmaker
Proxenito	Matchmaker in arranged marriages

Glossary

Rizogalo	Rice pudding
Simbetheri	The parents of your son-in-law or daughter-in-law
Skordalia	Garlic dip
Souvlaki	Chicken and lamb skewers
Stefana	Crowns used at an Orthodox wedding ceremony
Tarama	Fish roe dip
Thea	Aunty
Theo	Uncle
Trapezi	Table ladened with food
Tzatziki	Yoghurt and cucumber dip
Xeni	Outsiders
Xeno	Outsider
Xero di mana sou	I know your mother
Yiayia	Grandmother
Yiayia & Pappou	Grandparents
Zoni	Sash
Zorba, Kalamatianos, Syrtos, Zembekiko	Greek Style Dances

ABOUT THE AUTHOR

Dora De Laat was born in Adelaide, South Australia. Dora considers her family to be most important to her. Growing up as the youngest of six girls, Dora was the first in her family to go to university. As a first-generation student, she forged a path into higher education paving the way for others in her family to follow. Nonetheless, it was challenging to feel she belonged in a place that no one else in her family had been. This is Dora's first book about her childhood, growing up in a strict Cypriot household and her journey of falling in love. It stands as a lasting legacy for her family. Dora lives in Brisbane with her husband of forty years, enjoys activities such as reading, writing, travelling the world and most of all cherishing precious moments with her three beautiful grandchildren and her family.

ACKNOWLEDGEMENTS

Thank you to the incredible team at Ultimate 48 Hour Author, whose unwavering support and expertise transformed my dream of becoming a published author into a reality. Your dedication to this project was remarkable, and I am deeply grateful for your guidance throughout this journey.

In addition to my publishing team, I acknowledge and thank my family and friends for their significant roles in my life and the creation of this book. Your presence and wisdom have had a profound impact on me and I am grateful for your unwavering support and assistance during the writing of this book. Your belief in me fueled my determination to see this project through.

To my daughter Mia, your unwavering encouragement and belief in my abilities were the catalyst for embarking on this incredible journey. Your faith in me never wavered, and I am grateful for your inspiration.

Thank you, my cherished family and friends.

Mum and Dad, 1946

My earliest photo at
4 years old, 1967

Me, Dad and Liz, 1967

At our house in Woodville
Gardens, 1968

Holding my niece Anthea
in Brisbane, 1973

The six sisters. L to R: Mary, me, Helen, Liz, Angie and Louisa in Adelaide, 1970

And with Mum and Dad in Brisbane, 1996

Young love – Me and Tony, 1982

Pinning of the money tradition at our wedding, 1983

With my Maid of Honour Cathy and my Flower Girl Marey, 1983

Tony and his Best Man Jack, 1983

Me and Dad at his 90th Birthday, 2010

Me and my beautiful Mum, 2013

This Disowned Daughter

Me and my Thea Tsappou

Me and Tony over the years

Me, Mia and Tony, 2011

Andrew, Tony and Me, 2012

Me and Tony on our travels

Thailand, 2008

Hawaii, 2011

Bali, 2012

Hawaii, 2011

England, 2015

Cyprus, 2015

Santorini, 2015

Vietnam, 2018

Vietnam, 2018

Bali with our Koumbari Harry and Anthea

Vietnam with our Koumbari, 2018

United States, 2023

Tony, me, Andy and Angie, 2015

L to R: Desi, Cathy, Sophie, Thea Tsappou
Top: Me and Tony, 2014

Sally & Andrew's Wedding, 2012

Mia & Paul's Wedding, 2014

Me and Tony with our grandchildren, Tiarnah, Harlan and Nylah

This Disowned Daughter

Dad, me and Mum at my 18th Birthday, 1981

This Disowned Daughter

www.ingramcontent.com/pod-product-compliance
Lightning Source LLC
Chambersburg PA
CBHW030117100526
44591CB00009B/433